JODEL
SOLO
CHOR
1. DÖT CHUNNT HILF UND ROHT.
2. DÖT CHUNNT HILF UND ROHT.
3. DÖT CHUNNT HILF UND ROHT.
SOLO
CHOR
SOLO
CHOR
1.
2.

Peter Roth, *Psalm 148*.

Resonances: Klanghaus Toggenburg

Edited by Erol Doguoglu, Mirjam Fischer, and Astrid Staufer

Lars Müller Publishers

Table of Contents

Foreword

Erol Doguoglu

"I wanted to find an answer to the question of how architecture and music could come together at all."

Marcel Meili (1953–2019)

There is probably no building owner that has such a diverse portfolio as the public sector. After all, the variety of uses of its buildings is an illustration of the responsibilities of the state, and yet despite, or perhaps because of this, we are repeatedly surprised by the items in this collection. One example of such a surprise is the Klanghaus in Toggenburg. Who could have imagined that such a special building would land in the portfolio of the Canton of St.Gallen?

When the public sector builds, there is usually a focus on notions such as suitability, user-orientation, lifecycle costs, or flexibility. And yet, despite this, the canton comes up with a Klanghaus? But that which could initially seem surprising is, in reality, only logical. An idea that originated from the heart of the canton, a small, growing seedling that endured an eventful history, navigated all democratically necessary processes, and is now built reality. The Klanghaus is a statement from the Cultural Region of Toggenburg that is becoming a place for encountering an inherent aspect of our history and identity: sound.

It is impressive to learn how the architect Marcel Meili searched for the answer to the question cited at the start of this foreword by transforming his propositions into the Klanghaus, and, in doing so, one arrives at the unavoidable conclusion that any discovery is inseparable from the process of searching for it. He found a form that not just followed function, but much more than this, was also shaped by his intuition and by the experiences of his "journey to the heart of Swiss traditional music that wasn't planned as such."

This is why the Klanghaus has not become a purely functional machine but, rather, as the architect Eileen Gray described successful buildings, a "shell of man, his extension, his release, his spiritual emanation." Our shared history and cultural identity must and should be able to emanate.

They contribute to our self-image as a society. This is precisely why cultural buildings such as the Klanghaus rightfully belong in a public portfolio.

On this note, I would like to warmly welcome the Klanghaus to the family of buildings in the Canton of St.Gallen. Marcel Meili and the team led by Staufer & Hasler have made a place for us in which architecture and music can truly come together. We are looking forward to many encounters between the building and the sound.

Editorial Note

Mirjam Fischer

The Klanghaus Toggenburg is a place where one experiences a unique synergy between architecture, sound, and nature. As a "framework for projection or crystallization," it offers a range of approaches developed from many different perspectives. Like the project itself, this publication can also be seen as a research-based experiment that seeks to uncover new insights from a wide variety of specialist fields. The building emerged from the nine propositions prepared by Marcel Meili for the Thesis Competition in 2010.

The first part of the publication focuses on architectural aspects and constructional solutions that deliver extraordinary acoustic effects. In conversations with the sound artist Andres Bosshard and the acoustician Martin Lachmann, Sabine von Fischer explores how the landscape and natural echo are drawn into the interior and how the central space of the Klanghaus enters into a dialogue with its visitors with the help of bronze acoustic mirrors. In his concept for this central space, Marcel Meili was inspired by the rich and perforated ornamentation of the music room in the Ali Qapu Palace in Isfahan. Axel Langer pursues these similarities and illustrates how this ornamentation becomes a visible expression of the essence of the space and the architecture that goes far beyond its acoustic function. Eva Kuss sheds light on the interaction between space, sound, and structure and offers us an introduction to—and a tour of—all the key constructive and sound-specific aspects of the building and of its timber construction. From the starting point of instrument making, Matthias Ruf shows us how the resonance of the Klanghaus is created with the help of specially developed acoustic objects, and how the wooden building is made to vibrate and, thus, becomes a walkable instrument.

The second part is devoted to cultural and social questions. Andrea Wiegelmann describes the eventful twenty-year-long development process that preceded the realization of the Klanghaus as an essentially social project that could never have been completed without its innumerable protagonists. Christian Gressbach identifies resonance tourism as providing an opportunity for a soft and sustainable tourism that emerges in harmony with the landscape and the musical traditions of the Toggenburg Region. Alfred Messerli offers us surprising insights into Ulrich Bräker—who is otherwise well-known for his autobiographical notes "The Poor Man of Toggenburg"—and into his passionate interest in the region's folkloristic singing culture. For Lea Hagmann and Sonja Lieberherr-Schnyder, the focus is natural yodeling. They pass on the insights of Annelies Huser and Christian Metzler, who tell us what the locals think about Toggenburg's natural yodeling, what they themselves associate with it, and why yodeling is more than just a style of singing. Susanna Koeberle's investigation begins with Ruedi Vetsch and the 110,000 shingles that he made for the Klanghaus. Her investigation of his craft sheds a particular light on the material vitality of shingles. Finally, Astrid Staufer reflects upon the experimental character of the Klanghaus by looking back on the history of the planning process and—with a view to its future—asks what it means to build possibilities for the "experiment" that was initiated by Marcel Meili.

While Viviane Sonderegger's lyrically acrobatic contribution pays linguistic and philological homage to the Klanghaus, Peter Roth's scores and Christian Zehnder's soundlines provide the book with its acoustic parentheses. Ladina Bischof and Ueli Steingruber approach the Klanghaus in the form of some highly individual and atmospherically dense series of images and, in doing so, activate all our senses so that we can truly experience this very special timber building.

The insightful and richly illustrated essays bring to light some surprising outcomes and productive relationships and present, in the publication that has been precisely and painstakingly designed by Norm, an exceptionally multi-voiced and diverse portrait of the Klanghaus Toggenburg.

Resonances: Klanghaus Toggenburg demonstrates not only the way in which a public building of this sort can create a sense of identity for a region, but also the remarkable fascination that it can awaken far beyond that region's borders.

Thesis Competition

Public procurement in Switzerland envisages a range of possible tender procedures for building contracts. These are generally competitive processes that take the form of architectural competitions, which are open and anonymous or organized with a preliminary prequalification round based on reference projects. However, the design of the Klanghaus Toggenburg was such an open-ended and pioneering assignment that a special tender procedure was selected: a thesis competition. This involves the submission not of the usual finished project but, rather, of a series of design propositions and initial sketches that leave enormous scope for further development in dialogue with the organizers and users of the building following the selection of the winning proposal.

The Klanghaus is a place in which a series of spaces are superimposed upon each other: rural, acoustic, and architectural. Participants were required to develop propositions that addressed the relationships between architecture and sound and between architecture and landscape.

The commissioner was Canton St.Gallen, represented by the Baudepartement (Department of Building). The process was led by the Hochbauamt (Building Construction Office) of Canton St.Gallen. The thesis competition was organized as a selective process. The submitted documents were limited to ten A4 pages that were required to exclusively present, illustrate, and explain the design strategy (thesis).

In December 2009, following the receipt of ninety submissions that responded to the invitation to tender, the jury recommended that the client should invite six applicants and one substitute to participate in the thesis competition. Alongside Meili, Peter Architekten, these were SANAA, Miller & Maranta, Caruso St John Architects, Steven Holl Architects, and Snøhetta. Graber Pulver Architekten, who were later commissioned by the Klangwelt to design the reception building for the Klanghaus, the Resonanz-

The following pages contain the competition project of Marcel Meili.

Marcel Meili, “Neun Thesen und eine persönliche Nachbemerkung zum Entwurf für das Klanghaus Toggenburg,” in Hochbauamt des Kantons St.Gallen, Amt für Kultur, Kanton St.Gallen, *Klanghaus Toggenburg. Thesenkonkurrenz/Thesis Competition. Bericht des Preisgerichts/Report of the Jury*, 2010.

Authors: Marcel Meili, Meili, Peter Architekten, Zurich; Günther Vogt, landscape architect, Zurich; Andres Bosshard, musician and sound artist, Zurich; Martin Hess, producer and events organizer for traditional music, Obwalden/Zurich; Martin Lachmann, acoustician, Applied Acoustics, Gelterkinden; Martin Heller, exhibition designer, Zurich/Linz.

Key discussion partners: Edi Gasser, composer, Giswil; Toni Büeler, lead yodeler, Muotatal; Frowin Neff, yodeler, Appenzell; Alois Gabriel, Volksmusikhaus, Altdorf; Peter Berchtold, music teacher, Giswil; Willi Valotti, accordion player, Nesslau; Erika Stucky, musician, accordion player, Thalwil/Wallis; Dieter Ringli, ethnomusicologist, Seegräben.

Fig. 1

Fig. 1
Klanghaus on the Schwendisee.

zentrum Peter Roth, which they realized in partnership with the architect Martina Hauser, were invited to participate as the substitute.

In comparison with the other submissions—and as a consequence of the enormous passion that he had developed for the music and landscape of Toggenburg—Marcel Meili and his interdisciplinary team formulated an unusually clear vision of the project. "It was their thesis that was able to most comprehensively convince the jury: due to their empathy for the task and the precise and sometimes surprising conclusions that this led to, but also due to their insightful investigation of the geographical and cultural location."[1]

Two long-standing professional companions and friends of Marcel Meili made valuable contributions as foundations for the project following the thesis competition: the landscape architect Günther Vogt, in his mediating role with the Federal Commission for the Protection of Nature and Cultural Heritage, and the civil engineer Jürg Conzett, with his concept for the road realignment and the construction of the new bridge.

1 *Thesis Competition* 2010, p. 17.

1 Investigations: Architecture and Music

The notion that an "architecture for music" must embrace the medium to the point of almost becoming an instrument itself is far from self-evident—and actually a threat to its nature. Every architecture, even if it is merely seeking to fulfill its purpose, must maintain a distance from its function, in order to respect the autonomy of that function—and its own. This is why the act of designing a "building for music" means defining and delimiting the interaction between discrete worlds.

Traditional music and jazz have at least one thing in common. In theory, they can emerge anywhere. Spaces for such music are not dependent upon reverberation times, insulation values, or coverage angles. In fact, the opposite tends to be the case: Both forms of music are responses to the specific characteristics of a place, to the atmosphere, the mood of the listeners and the musicians, and the sound of the surroundings. In other words, Klangwelten (Sound Worlds) can emerge just as easily in an improvised jam session in a garage. This is the strength of the project. Attempting to restrain this energy with the "helping hand of architecture" would be a huge mistake. But what does it mean to create a new architecture in which the musical project retains its autonomy and remains free to appropriate a place with the help of sound?

The history of buildings for music is long and richly varied, and it runs through every culture. Naturally, the way the sound resonates almost always plays a role. In addition to this, these buildings weave together atmospheric, dramaturgical, or spiritual levels of awareness in varying intensities to form a ritual, a mass, or a Gesamtkunstwerk—or they may take a step back, like the shell-shaped bandstand in the spa gardens. How close is the relationship between Klangwelten and their architecture?

Light is shed on this question by the pavilion at Expo 1958 designed by Le Corbusier and Xenakis where the "synthèse des arts" was taken to the point where music, space, color, proportion, and movement merged completely. The pavilion was arguably less a Gesamtkunstwerk than an impressive artwork that wove together a wide range of techniques, disciplines, and perceptions in the form of an installation. This indicates the limits for the Klanghaus: If the design explores the relationship between music and architecture, it does so as a place of free musical creation and not as an acoustic work of art. It will give the music space, rather than form. And as both a building and an image it will refrain from offering any prediction or evaluation of what will happen there. In other words, it is impossible to imagine a specific "architecture of Klangwelten."

Fig. 1
Büchel player in Muotatal.

Fig. 2
Philips Pavilion, 1958.

Fig. 3
Next to Schwendisee.

1 **Erkundungen: Architektur und Musik** Dass eine «Architektur für die Musik» sich dieser anzuschmiegen hat, bis sie selbst beinahe ein Instrument geworden ist, dies ist keineswegs selbstverständlich – eher schon bedrohlich. Jede Architektur, auch wenn sie ihren Zweck sucht, wird zu ihrem Gebrauch Distanz einhalten, um die Autonomie des Gebrauchs zu wahren – und ihre eigene. Ein «Haus für Musik» zu entwerfen, bedeutet deshalb, die Berührungen eigenständiger Welten zu bestimmen und zu begrenzen.

Büchelbläser Muotatal

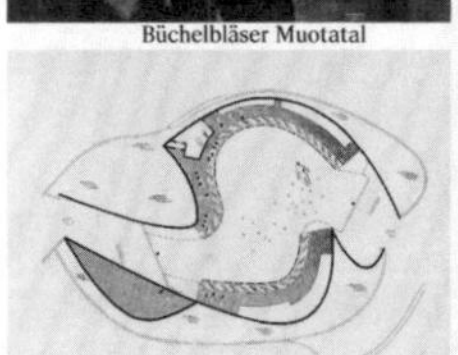

Philips Pavillon 1958

Beim Schwendisee

In zumindest einer Eigenschaft berühren sich die Volksmusik und der Jazz. Theoretisch kann diese Musik irgendwo entstehen. Der Raum dieser Musik ist nicht von Nachhallzeiten, Isolationswerten und Abstrahlwinkeln abhängig. Eher ist es umgekehrt: Beide Musikformen sind Antworten auf die besonderen Eigenschaften eines Orts, auf seine Stimmung, auf jene der Zuhörer und Musiker, auf den Klang der Umgebung. Klangwelten könnten sich also in einer Garage entwickeln wie eine improvisierte Jam-Session. Das ist eine Stärke des Projekts. Diese Kraft durch «architektonische Fürsorge» zu bändigen wäre ein grosser Fehler.

Was heisst es aber, in einer neuen Architektur dem musikalischen Projekt seine Autonomie zu belassen, die Freiheit zu wahren, sich einen Ort durch Klang anzueignen?

Die Geschichte der Architekturen für Musik ist reich und alt, und sie verteilt sich auf alle Kulturen. Natürlich, der Widerhall des Tons spielt fast immer eine Rolle. Darüber hinaus verschränken diese Bauten in unterschiedlicher Dichte atmosphärische, dramaturgische oder spirituelle Wahrnehmungsformen bis zum Ritual, zur Messe oder zum Gesamtkunstwerk – oder sie ziehen sich als Gerät zurück, wie die Orchestermuschel im Kurpark. Wie nahe kommen sich die Klangwelten und ihre Architektur?

Erhellend dafür ist der Pavillon der Expo 1958 von Le Corbusier und Xenakis. Denn er hat die «synthèse des arts» an einen Punkt getrieben, wo Musik, Raum, Farbe, Proportion und Bewegung völlig ineinander verschmelzen. Der Pavillon war wohl weniger ein Gesamtkunstwerk als ein eindrückliches Kunstwerk, das verschiedenste Techniken, Disziplinen und Wahrnehmungsformen wie in einer Installation verwoben hat.

Der Pavillon verweist auf die Grenzen für das Klanghaus: Wenn der Entwurf über das Verhältnis von Musik und Architektur nachdenkt, dann als Ort einer freien musikalischen Arbeit und nicht als Ton-Kunstwerk. Er wird der Musik Raum geben, nicht Form. Und er wird sich als Bauwerk, auch als Bild, jeder Vorhersage oder Bewertung darüber enthalten, was dort passieren wird.

Lässt sich die «Architektur der Klangwelten» also als etwas Spezifisches gar nicht vorstellen?

Marcel Meili, *«Neun Thesen und eine persönliche Nachbemerkung zum Entwurf für das Klanghaus Toggenburg»*, in *Thesenkonkurrenz*, 2010.

2 Investigations: Authenticity

“Authenticity” is probably the only term that will be used equally by all the musicians who will perform in the Klanghaus. Interpreted as “realness” or “historical truth,” the term remains hollow. However, traditional and other “lowbrow” forms of music share the concept of authenticity as a way of “being with oneself.” The Klanghaus will provide a space for enjoying the intimacy of such experiences.

Today’s traditional Swiss music is less than 150 years old. This means that it is hardly a suitable medium for anchoring music in the country’s history. But this observation is not relevant. The much more revealing question is: How could a musical form that is capable of establishing such a profound sense of identity evolve in such a short time?

When we speak of traditional musicians, we quickly realize that terms like “authenticity” or “Swissness” are concealing something deeper. We become aware of a complex emotional framework that operates at many different scales: the individual biography, daily life, the valley as home, or music as an intuitive language. Traditional music communicates a sense of identity less through its history than through its ability to allow these experiences to surface—to create an atmosphere in which the musicians can “find themselves.”

This is perhaps clearest in the case of yodelers. Yodeling is an extraordinarily emotional and physical form of music: The yodel appears to flourish deep within the sound of their voice. When yodelers speak about their music, we are reminded of old blues musicians. These are artists whose music offers a fundamental experience that is intuitively emotional and less influenced by the external appearance of a place than by their own voice, by the interaction or by the audience. For the yodeler, these are the moments in which the music becomes “real.”

The Klanghaus is the place where we can seek moments in which musical cultures encounter one other. Our experience of natural tones intersects with our curiosity about elementary “alien” sounds. This is why the Klanghaus is not a concert hall but, rather, the setting for a somewhat introverted dialogue that takes place within the music itself. Authenticity is the space where diverse styles can come together.

But what does this mean for the architecture?

The Klanghaus is an open vessel. The architecture neither interferes nor imposes direction. The building is neither an acoustic installation nor an event space. It unfolds its own expressive possibilities in the background like a protective shell around the experiment. As architecture, it allows the senses to be engaged in just the same way as music. It undoubtedly sets its own tone, because it is a place where the two worlds converge. And this, too, is architecture, because architecture always resonates.

Fig. 1
Blues guitarist, Washington, D. C.

Fig. 2
Balthasar Streiff Gruppe.

Fig. 3
Noldi Alder, yodeler.

2 **Erkundungen: Authentizität**

«Authentizität» ist wahrscheinlich der einzige Begriff, der von allen Musikern gleichermassen in Anspruch genommen werden wird, die im Klanghaus Musik machen werden. Als «Echtheit» oder «historische Wahrheit» bliebe der Begriff leere Formel. Was aber Volksmusiken mit anderen Musikformen «von unten» verbindet, ist Authentizität als eine Form des «Bei-sich-selber-sein». Das Klanghaus wird der Intimität dieser Erfahrung einen Raum geben.

Bluesgitarrist Washington DC

Balthasar Streiff Gruppe

Noldi Alder, Jodler

Die Schweizer Volksmusik von heute ist keine 150 Jahre alt. Sie eignet sich somit kaum, die Musik in der nationalen Geschichte zu verankern. Aber diese Feststellung ist uninteressant. Aufschlussreich ist die Frage, wie sich in beschränkter Zeit eine Musik herausbilden konnte, welche so tiefliegende Identitäten begründet.

Spricht man mit Volksmusikern, so spürt man bald, dass sich hinter Formeln wie «Echtheit» oder «Schweizertum» noch etwas anderes verbirgt. Es zeichnet sich ein vielschichtiges emotionales Gefüge in unterschiedlichen Massstäben ab: die eigene Biografie, der konkrete Alltag, das Tal als Heimat, Musik als intuitive Sprache. Identität vermittelt die Volksmusik weniger durch ihre Geschichte, sondern eher, weil in ihr diese Erfahrungen zur Deckung gelangen: Eine Stimmung, in der die Musiker «zu sich selber finden».

Am deutlichsten wird dies wohl bei den Jodlerinnen und Jodlern. Jodeln ist eine aussergewöhnlich emotionale, körperliche Musik: der Jodler scheint im Innern des Klangs seiner Stimme aufzugehen. Wenn Jodler über Ihre Musik sprechen, dann erinnert dies an einen alten Blueser: Es geht um eine gefühlsbezogene Grunderfahrung, die von Äusserlichkeiten des Orts weniger beeinflusst ist als von der eigenen Stimmung, vom Zusammenspiel, vom Publikum. In solchen Momenten wird für den Jodler die Musik «echt».

Das Klanghaus ist der Ort, wo dieser Moment in der Begegnung von musikalischen Kulturen gesucht wird. Die Erfahrung des Naturtons überlagert sich mit der Neugierde an elementaren Klängen des «Fremden». Deshalb ist das Klanghaus kein Konzerthaus, sondern der Ort eines eher introvertierten Gesprächs im Innern der Musik. Authentizität ist die Ebene, auf der verschiedene Stile zusammenfinden.

Doch was heisst das für die Architektur?

Das Klanghaus ist ein offenes Gefäss. Die Architektur mischt sich nicht ein und führt nicht. Sie ist keine Klanginstallation und kein Eventraum. Sie breitet ihre eigenen Möglichkeiten des Ausdrucks im Hintergrund des Raums aus als Schale um das Experiment. Sie kümmert sich als Architektur um die Entfaltung der Sinne, wie es die Musik tut. Und ohne Zweifel: Sie nimmt sich ihres eigenen Tons an, weil dort die beiden Welten aufeinandertreffen. Doch auch das ist Architektur, denn Architektur klingt immer.

3 Investigations: Three Lines on Music

The music and the building in which it resides approach, touch, and intertwine in three spheres: the sound of the building, the atmosphere of its spaces, and the presence of the surrounding landscape. It is here—and only here—that the architecture seeks a direct dialogue with the music.

Architecture resonates in one way or another. The building is the resonating body for all the sounds produced within it. But how can the tone of the architecture be configured if the music is open and unpredictable? No, the building cannot be tuned to match the music as if creating a space for a chamber orchestra. Quite the opposite: The architecture will generate its own rich array of sounds, harmonized as in the salon, a church, or on the field below the rock face. Music encounters the sound of an object.

The architectural atmosphere of the spaces follows this approach. Paradoxically, one condition for an effortless encounter between architecture and music is provided by the "garage image": The recognition that the musical event that will take place here could happen anywhere. The music requires no architectural empathy, but rather an atmosphere of openness, lightness, and even spatial provocation. The musicians should feel welcome, perhaps in the same way as they would in a country inn. But beyond this, the spaces avoid ingratiating themselves with the music, and the architecture keeps its secret.

The key to the relationship between music and architecture lies in the landscape. Perhaps it is untrue that traditional music in Switzerland plays "before the backdrop of the impressive mountains." Perhaps instead, it confronts the mountains and resonates towards the cliff face. Musicians from the city have the same feeling, because they are more than just "overwhelmed": They begin to see their music as a response to the power of the rocks. The impact of the landscape is the essential experience that will be shared, wordlessly, by all the musicians who work here.

This encounter between the music and the mountains echoes in the architecture. As a human-made object, architecture is obliged to compete with the nature of the mountains, whether it takes the form of a farmhouse, a mountain hut, or a church. Architecture is that "machine à émouvoir," whose form enables us to sense, grasp, and assess its presence in the landscape—almost like an artificial echo of nature.

Fig. 1
H.-J. Sommer in the church.

Fig. 2
An inn in Toggenburg.

Fig. 3
View towards Schafberg.

3 **Erkundungen:**
Drei Linien zur Musik

In drei Sphären kommen sich die Musik und das Haus, das sie beherbergt, nahe, sie berühren sich, sie verschränken sich: Im Klang des Hauses, in der Stimmung der Räume und in der Präsenz der Landschaft, in der das Haus steht. Hier – nur hier – sucht die Architektur den direkten Dialog mit der Musik.

H.-J. Sommer in der Kirche

Beiz im Toggenburg

Zum Schafberg

Architektur klingt, so oder so. Das Haus ist der Resonanzkörper aller Töne, die hier erzeugt werden. Aber worauf stellt sich der architektonische Klang ein, wenn die Musik offen und unvorhersehbar ist? Nein, der Klang des Hauses kann nicht auf die Musik abgestimmt werden wie für ein Kammerorchester. Eher ist es umgekehrt: Die Architektur wird den Reichtum ihrer eigenen Klänge entwerfen, warm, breit, abgestimmt. Auf diese unsichtbaren Eigenschaften wird die Musik stossen, sie wird sie entdecken wie im Säli, in der Kirche oder auf der Wiese unter der Felswand. Musik begegnet dem Klang eines Gegenstandes.

Die **architektonische Stimmung der Räume** folgt dieser Spur. Voraussetzung für eine souveräne Begegnung zwischen Architektur und Musik bildet paradoxerweise das «Garagen-Bild»: jene Erkenntnis also, dass überall geschehen könnte, was hier musikalisch passieren wird. Die Musik bedarf keiner architektonischen Anteilnahme, aber einer Atmosphäre der Offenheit, auch Leichtigkeit, selbst der räumlichen Provokation. Die Musiker sollen sich willkommen fühlen, wie in einem Landgasthof vielleicht. Sonst aber versagen sich die Räume jede Anbiederung an die Musik, die Architektur bewahrt sich ihr Geheimnis.

Der Schlüssel zur Beziehung zwischen Musik und Architektur ist die **Landschaft.** Vielleicht ist es gar nicht so, dass die Volksmusik in der Schweiz «vor der Kulisse der eindrücklichen Berge» spielt. Vielleicht tritt sie eher gegen die Berge an, hallt den Felsen entgegen. Von diesem Gefühl wird auch der Musiker aus der Stadt ergriffen, denn er ist nicht bloss «überwältigt»: Er beginnt sich seine Musik als Antwort auf die Wucht der Felsen vorzustellen. Die Wirkung der Landschaft ist jene elementare Erfahrung, welche alle Musiker, die hier arbeiten werden, ohne jedes Wort verbinden wird.

Diese Begegnung der Musik mit den Bergen hat einen Widerhall in der Architektur. Als vom Mensch gemachter Körper muss Architektur in einen Widerstreit mit der Natur der Berge treten, sei es als Hof, als Berghütte oder als Kirche. Die Architektur ist jene «machine à émouvoir», welche durch ihre Form die Präsenz in der Landschaft als Wahrnehmung vermittelt, greifbar macht, gewichtet, fast wie ein künstliches Echo der Natur.

4 Investigations: Klangwelten—a Project

The Klangwelten do not constitute an institution, nor are they Swiss, nor dedicated to traditional music. They are a project—a musical project with an author and a setting. They are the source of an idea that radiates far and wide and, at their heart, a point on the map that aspires to become a "magic place"—perhaps, someday, like Monte Verità or St. Yves. This attachment to a specific place opens the project to critique—but this is precisely its strength.

If you move in traditional-music circles you encounter a certain reticence towards the Klangwelten. This is hardly surprising for a project dedicated to exploring the margins of a culture that has more than its fair share of inertia. Yet the idea is confidently rooted in traditional music. It has an almost anthropological faith in the power of the acoustic experience and in a universal musicality whose origins are embedded in popular tradition. This is why the authors of the research do not capitulate to free experimentalism, but rather base their work on rigorous hypotheses: the pan-cultural dependability of the natural tone, the dimension of an imaginable spirituality, or the fundamental emotional experience of multisensory perception.

This suggests that the project should be understood more as an oversized acoustic installation than as an organization—and this has implications for the building that houses this "eternal resonance." It will avoid all the symbolism of a musical institution. After all, the Klanghaus is the formal and physical embodiment of a musical experiment, and nothing more.

In this sense, the Klangwelten are an unusual example of work at the margins of traditional music. The power of renewal that emanates from such music—which is not so common—is primarily generated by the virtuosity of gifted and curious younger musicians or idiosyncratic individualists. Above all, these young instrumentalists are much better trained than their parents. They experimentally test the boundaries of their instruments and work at the margins of free music or under the influence of other ethnic traditions, sometimes with phenomenal musical results. These are voyages of exploration to the very heart of music itself, dedicated to the joy of musical discovery.

On the other hand, the Klangwelten also convey much more clearly defined intrinsic motifs that emphasize the almost existential dimension of acoustic perception. This broad definition of music evokes a "worldview" in which architecture, landscape, and music combine to create a fundamentally archaic experience of sensuality.

Fig. 1
Elderly yodeler, Toggenburg.

Fig. 2
Mary Wigman, Monte Verità.

Fig. 3
Klangwelten Toggenburg.

4 **Erkundungen: Klangwelten – ein Projekt**

Klangwelten ist keine Institution, schon gar keine schweizerische, und auch keine für die Volksmusik. Sie ist ein Projekt – ein musikalischer Entwurf, der einen Autor hat und einen Ort. Von hier aus strahlt eine Idee aus, und im Zentrum möchte sich ein Punkt auf der Landkarte zum «magischen Ort» verwandeln – vielleicht einmal wie der Monte Verità oder St. Yves. Diese Beschlagnahmung eines Ortes durch die Idee macht das Projekt angreifbar – aber gerade darin liegt seine Stärke.

Alte Jodlerin, Toggenburg

Mary Wigman, Monte Verità

Klangwelten Toggenburg

Hört man sich in der Volksmusik um, so begegnet man einiger Zurückhaltung gegenüber den Klangwelten. Das ist nicht verwunderlich, wenn ein Projekt sich die Erkundung der Ränder einer Kultur vornimmt, der viel Beharrungsvermögen innewohnt. Doch die Idee ist sich ihres Zentrums in der Volksmusik sicher. Sie verlässt sich in fast anthropologischem Vertrauen auf die Kraft der Klangerfahrung und auf eine universelle Musikalität, deren Ursprünge in der Volkstradition gebunden sind. Die forschende Arbeit liefert sich deshalb nicht einem freien Experimentalismus aus. Die Autoren legen ihr strenge Hypothesen zugrunde: die pankulturelle Verbindlichkeit des Naturtons etwa, die Dimension einer denkbaren Spiritualität, die emotionale Grunderfahrung einer alle Sinne umfassenden Wahrnehmung.

Dies legt es nahe, das Projekt eher wie eine übergrosse klangliche Installation zu verstehen denn wie eine Organisation. Für das Haus dieses «endlosen Klingens» hat dies Folgen: Es wird alle Zeichen einer musikalischen Institution vermeiden. Letztlich ist das Klanghaus der formale und physische Körper eines musikalischen Experiments, nur das.

Klangwelten stellt mit dieser Idee einen aussergewöhnlichen Fall im Rahmen der Grenzarbeiten der Volksmusik dar. Deren Erneuerungsenergien aus ihrem Innern – die nicht allzu zahlreich sind – werden meist von der Virtuosität begabter und neugieriger Musiker der jüngeren Generation oder von eigenwilligen Einzelgängern getragen. Sie sind vor allem sehr viel besser ausgebildete Instrumentalisten als ihre Väter. Ihre Arbeit experimentiert an der Grenze der Instrumente, an den Rändern zur freien Musik oder unter Einfluss anderer Ethnomusik, teils mit überragenden musikalischen Resultaten. Es sind Entdeckungsreisen im Innern der Musik selbst – um das Vergnügen der musikalischen Entdeckung willen.

In den Klangwelten dagegen scheinen deutlich klarer konturierte ideelle Motive durch, welche die beinahe existenzielle Dimension der Klangwahrnehmung hervorheben. Ein so umfassender Musikbegriff trägt die Züge einer «Welt-Wahrnehmung»: Architektur, Landschaft und Musik verschränken sich in einer archaischen Grunderfahrung von Sinnlichkeit.

5 Investigations: The Sound of the Landscape

The landscape is key. This is the Toggenburg, which gives the acoustic experiment a set of coordinates—both aural and topographical. The sound becomes spatial, and the landscape resonates. The relationship is two-sided: the music listens and responds. The Klanghaus acts like an energized membrane between the musicians and the valley. Can architecture achieve this?

All architecture is an artificial installation that reconciles our perceptions of a concrete place and of nature. And every building does this in both directions, as a transformation of the landscape and as a place that encapsulates the impressions of that landscape. This becomes particularly clear in the mountains: The route to the hut reveals the topography, the building defines the location and establishes orientations that were previously hidden, the space captures the view, and silence and sounds are separated. All these characteristics can amplify the impact of architecture and give intense and unmistakable form to the dialogue between landscape and music.

The mountains of Upper Toggenburg are the home of the musical project and, more broadly, the home of the many musicians who are guests here. All the musicians with whom we have spoken, whether traditional or experimental, are certain that this landscape will leave traces in their music. This is the line of action along which architecture can unfold its potential: The landscape is "drawn into the spaces"—not just for the eyes, but also in terms of sound or smell.

The question becomes even stranger when one reverses the direction: The Klanghaus will be visible from a great distance—but will the sounds also find their way back into the landscape? The building dreams of being like the projection in the rock face, where we hear the landscape particularly well—and where we can be heard most clearly down in the valley when we shout.

Every landscape resonates, just as all architecture does. And every landscape carries the sound of someone calling in an unmistakable way, just as it carries the Alpine blessing or the clapping of the child playing with the echo. Everyone with whom we have spoken dreams of playing outside up here. But is there an architecture that receives sounds especially clearly and transmits them particularly well?

It's called a "membrane": the architecture is a gently oscillating, sensitively reacting skin between the "outside" and the "inside," between music and landscape, acting like an amplifier to maximize the interpenetration of space and landscape. An architecture that consolidates and intensifies the senses.

Fig. 1
Parlor in Alphubel.

Fig. 2
Yodeler in Appenzell.

Fig. 3
Lai da Vons Hütte.

5 **Erkundungen: Der Klang der Landschaft**

Die Landschaft ist der Schlüssel. Es ist das Toggenburg, durch welches das akustische Experiment einen Koordinatenpunkt erhält, akustisch wie topografisch. Der Klang wird räumlich und die Landschaft klingt. Die Beziehung wird zweiseitig: Die Musik hört und antwortet. Das Klanghaus wird wie eine angeregte Membran zwischen den Musikern und dem Talraum liegen. Kann Architektur das leisten?

Stube am Alphubel

Jodler im Appenzell

Lai da Vons Hütte

Jede Architektur ist eine künstliche Installation, welche die Wahrnehmung zwischen einem konkreten Ort und der Natur vermittelt. Und jedes Haus tut dies in beide Richtungen, als Veränderung der Landschaft und als Ort, der Eindrücke der Landschaft zusammenfasst. Besonders anschaulich wird dies in den Bergen: Der Weg zur Hütte ordnet die Topografie, das Haus gewichtet den Ort und legt Richtungen fest, die zuvor verborgen waren, der Raum fasst den Ausblick, Stille und Geräusch werden getrennt. All diese Eigenschaften kann Architektur schärfen, sie kann dem Dialog zwischen Landschaft und Musik ein intensives und unverwechselbares Profil verleihen.

Die Berge des oberen Toggenburg sind die Heimat des musikalischen Projekts, im weiteren Sinne aber auch die Heimat vieler Musiker, die hier Gäste sind. Alle Musiker, mit denen wir gesprochen haben, ob Volksmusiker oder Experimentelle, sind sich sicher, dass diese Landschaft in ihrer Musik Spuren hinterlassen wird. Auf dieser Wirkungslinie wird Architektur Potenzial entfalten können: Die Landschaft «in die Räume hineintragen» – nicht nur für die Augen, sondern durch den Ton oder den Geruch.

Sehr viel ungewöhnlicher wird die Frage, wenn sich die Richtung umdreht: Sichtbar wird das Klanghaus von weit her sein – aber gelangen auch Töne zurück in die Landschaft? Das Haus träumt davon, wie jener Vorsprung in der Felswand zu sein, wo wir die Landschaft besonders gut hören können – und wo man uns besonders klar hört im Tal, wenn wir rufen.

Jede Landschaft klingt, genau wie jede Architektur. Und jede Landschaft trägt den Ton des Rufenden auf unverwechselbare Weise weiter wie den Alpsegen oder das Klatschen des Kindes, das mit dem Echo spielt. Und alle, mit denen wir gesprochen haben, träumen davon, hier oben «draussen zu spielen». Gibt es eine Architektur, welche Töne besonders klar empfängt und besonders gut wegträgt?

Das hiesse «Membran»: Die Architektur ist eine leicht schwingende, fein reagierende Haut zwischen «Aussen» und «Innen», zwischen Musik und Landschaft, die wie ein Verstärker wirkt, die grösstmögliche Durchdringung von Raum und Landschaft. Eine Architektur, die Sinne zusammenfasst und intensiviert.

6 Design: An Architectural Vocabulary

Can we imagine all of this as a concrete project? These sketches serve as a mental diagram. Their purpose is to record and test our findings through the language of architecture. The plan is no more than a formula for supporting this investigation: of the Klanghaus in the landscape and of its spatial characteristics. The final architecture could also look completely different.

6 **Entwurf: Eine architektonische Grammatik** Können wir uns all dies als konkretes Projekt vorstellen? Die Skizzen sind ein gedankliches Diagramm. Sie haben die Aufgabe, Erkenntnisse in die Sprache der Architektur zu fassen und zu prüfen. Der Plan ist nicht mehr als eine Formel für die Untersuchung: für das Klanghaus in der Landschaft und für die Eigenschaften der Räume. Eine spätere Architektur könnte auch ganz anders aussehen.

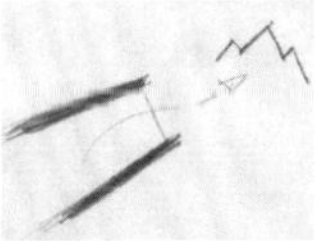

1. Nach dem Prinzip der Kamera fasst das Haus das Panorama in einzelne riesige Ausblicke.

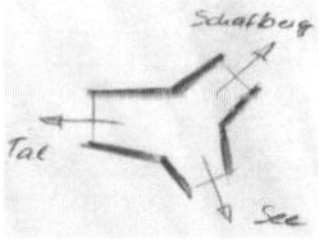

2. Die Blicke werden in die Sichtachsen der Landschaft gelegt: zum Schwendisee, zum Schafberg und in den Talausgang.

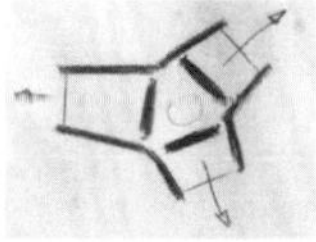

3. Es entsteht eine dreiarmige Struktur mit einem introvertierten Zentralraum und drei Flügeln, offen zur Landschaft.

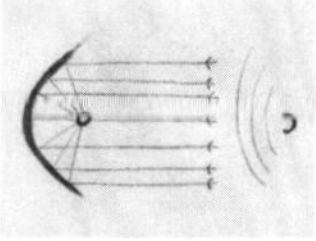

4. Die grosse Parabel ist in der Lage, Geräusche in ausserordentlicher Intensität zu sammeln und zusammenzuführen.

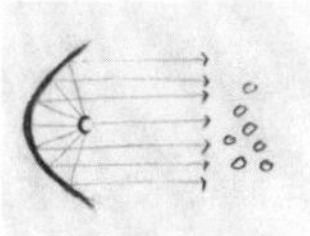

5. Die Parabel funktioniert auch umgekehrt: Sie trägt Klänge wie ein natürlicher Verstärker in die Landschaft.

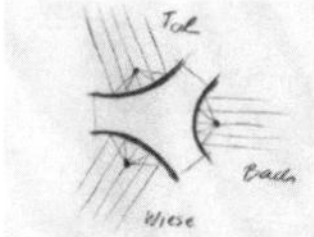

6. Die Parabeln scheiden drei Tonräume aus: Den Flur am See, die Nische beim Wasser und die Töne des Tals.

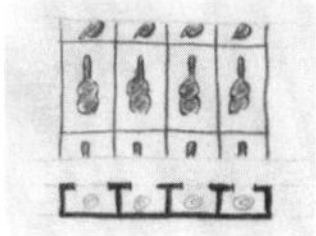

7. Die Akustik des Hauses wird über Holz kontrolliert. Drei Resonatoren-Tore beherrschen den Innenraum.

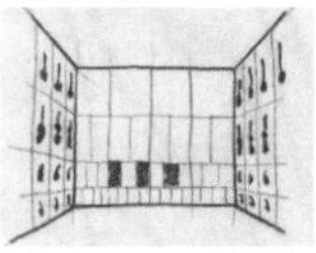

8. Die Resonatoren sind Teil eines Holztäfer-Netzes, das alle Räume umspannt, und akustisch weich macht.

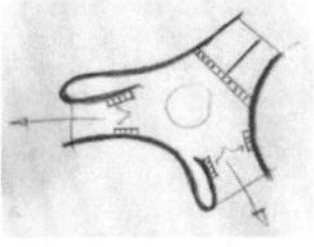

9. Diese Tore formen den verzogenen Sechseck-Saal. Sie können geöffnet werden, der Hauptraum wendet sich der Landschaft zu.

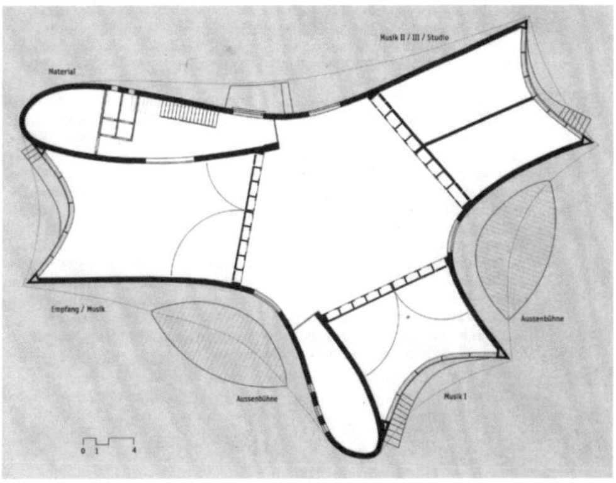

Fig. 1
The building employs the principle of the camera to capture the panorama in a series of distinct, wide-angle views.

Fig. 2
These views are aligned with the visual axes of the landscape: towards Schwendisee, Schafberg, and the foot of the valley.

Fig. 3
This creates a three-armed structure with an introverted central space and three wings that open outward to the landscape.

Fig. 4
The vast parabolic surface captures sounds and combines them to achieve an extraordinary intensity.

Fig. 5
The parabola also functions in reverse, emitting sounds into the landscape like a natural amplifier.

Fig. 6
These parabolas define three distinct acoustic spaces: the lakeside fields, the niche by the stream, and the sounds of the valley.

Fig. 7
The acoustics of the building are determined by the timber. Three resonance portals regulate the interior.

Fig. 8
These resonators are part of a grid of wooden panels that lines the spaces and softens the acoustics.

Fig. 9
The portals shape the elongated hexagonal space. They can be opened to allow the main space to engage with the landscape.

7 Design: A Membrane Facing the Landscape

When the Klanghaus is used as a place for making music, it opens up to the external landscape in several ways: visually, acoustically, and in the manner in which this landscape is experienced. In this respect, the architecture subtly orchestrates the encounter, structuring it and giving it both form and meaning. The intense dialogue between the landscape and the music is shaped by an open, gestural architecture—more than anywhere else.

Two sets of three axes—three visual axes and three acoustic axes—embed the project in the topography, structuring its position within Toggenburg.

Every point in the landscape has its own "hidden" axes. These are the alignments that one expects to find in that landscape and that one can sense at that specific point. The large windows are positioned on these axes: Wildhuser Schafberg, the line of the valley, and the basin of Schwendisee. The landscape is drawn in through—and accessed from—these "camera windows." When the windows are opened, the spaces transform into terraces.

The large parabolic walls are stretched between these wings. The remarkable acoustic performance of physical parabolas was first demonstrated in the early days of anti-aircraft defense, before they were replaced by electronic amplifiers. Dam walls also provide striking evidence of this effect. In the Klanghaus, the walls act as acoustic magnifiers that capture the sound of the landscape. And, as parabolas also function acoustically in both directions, they also act as open-air platforms for music. This is why stages are positioned in front of them. Transmission and reception intertwine.

The three acoustic reflectors serve the same role in the landscape as the camera windows. They carve three distinct spaces out of the topographical acoustic panorama: the intimate space by the stream, the basin of the lake, and the valley, with its human-made sounds.

The heavy wooden planks that form the walls will lend a warm hue to these sounds—adding depth to the mixture of Swiss and Mongolian yodeling echoing across the fields by the lake.

The smaller glass parabolas will generate another tone: clearer, harder, and more urban.

The curves give the building an amorphous geometry: everything is sight and sound. The planks of the parabolas follow the slope of the site like a hanging cloak—heavy timber that resembles fabric. In all these ways, the structure resists the image of a conventional building. The Klanghaus is a spatial and acoustic installation, whose meaning is not immediately apparent. It has to be discovered like an objet trouvé.

Fig. 1
Parabolic wall of the Klanghaus.

Fig. 2
View out into the valley.

Fig. 3
Acoustic radar, Dover, GB.

7 **Entwurf: Die Membran zur Landschaft** Im Gebrauch des Klanghauses als Ort der Musik erschliesst sich die Aussenwelt der Landschaft auf verschiedene Weise: durch die Sicht, durch die Töne, in der Art, wie sie betreten wird. In dieser Hinsicht beansprucht die Architektur eine heimliche Regie: Sie gewichtet, gibt der Begegnung Form und Bedeutung. Ein dichter Dialog zwischen Landschaft und Musik nimmt durch eine offene, gestische Architektur Gestalt an – mehr als irgendwo sonst.

Klanghaus Parabolwand

Blick talauswärts

Acustic radar, Dover GB

Zweimal drei Achsen legt der Entwurf in die Topografie, um seine Lage im Toggenburg zu ordnen: drei Sichtachsen und drei Klangachsen.

Jede Landschaft verfügt von jedem Punkt aus betrachtet über so etwas wie «verborgene» Achsen. Es sind die erahnten Fluchtlinien jenes Landschaftsraums, der an dieser Stelle wahrgenommen wird. Auf diese Achsen sind die riesigen Fenster ausgerichtet: Der Wildhuser Schafberg, die Talachse und die Kammer des Schwendisees. In diesen «Kamera-Fenstern» wird die Landschaft hineingezogen, und sie wird von dort aus betreten. Durch die Öffnung der Fenster werden die Räume zu Terrassen.

Zwischen diesen Flügeln werden die grossen Parabolwände aufgespannt. Gebaute Parabole haben ihre stupende akustische Leistungsfähigkeit einst in der Fliegerabwehr bewiesen, bevor sie durch elektronische Verstärker ersetzt worden sind. Staumauern legen von dieser Wirkung ein erstaunliches Zeugnis ab. Im Klanghaus werden die Wände wie akustische Lupen eingesetzt, beim Aufspüren der Töne der Landschaft. Weil Parabole akustisch aber auch in umgekehrter Richtung funktionieren, sind sie auch Bühnen für die Musik im Freien: Deshalb verfügen die Wände über vorgelagerte Plattformen. Senden und Empfangen greifen ineinander.

Die drei akustischen Reflektoren tun in der Landschaft das Gleiche wie die Kamera-Fenster. Sie schneiden aus dem landschaftlichen Klangpanorama drei Räume mit unterschiedlichen Eigenschaften aus: der intime Raum am Bach, das Seebecken und der Talraum mit seinen menschengemachten Geräuschen.

Die schweren Holzbohlen, welche die Wände formen, werden den Geräuschen eine warme Farbe verleihen – genau wie dem schweizerisch-mongolischen Jodelmix, der auf dem See-Flur hinaussingt. Die kleineren Glasparabeln werden einen anderen Ton erzeugen: klarer, härter, städtischer.

Die Kurven verleihen dem Gebäude eine amorphe Geometrie: Alles ist Sicht und Ton. Die Bohlen der Parabole folgen wie ein hängendes Gewand der Neigung des Terrains, schwere Hölzer, die wirken wie ein Stoff. In all diesen Aspekten verweigert die Konstruktion das Bild eines Hauses. Das Klanghaus ist eine räumliche und akustische Installation, deren Bedeutung nicht unmittelbar zutage tritt. Sie muss entdeckt werden wie ein Fundstück.

8 Design: The Sound of the Spaces—Architectural

The platform does not submit to the allure of absolute openness. The deeply complex and intense relationship with the landscape is the result of an architecture that maintains a balance between openness and intimacy. This is why the spaces also offer quiet, introverted moments that are reminiscent of a parlor. And yet, since the key spatial elements are flexible, they shift in character, as if they are on a stage.

The Klanghaus is a building entirely constructed of timber. It is this timber construction that allows for the configuration of a range of resonances, enabling the spaces to be precisely calibrated as they transition from openness to intimacy.

The heart of the building is a contemplative, introverted space. This focus highlights not only the music but also, paradoxically, the landscape. Similar to the small Romanesque churches in the mountains, it is the stillness and the composure of this space that accentuate the vastness of the landscape. The lateral elements, which come into play as soon as the resonance portals are opened, completely change the spatial effect and transform the building into a platform. These side wings act almost like catapults, launching the space into the landscape.

The homogeneous, woven surface of the wood paneling that covers the walls creates continuity between the different spaces. This strongly sculpted finish excels in spreading sound. The acoustics can be finely tuned by reducing or increasing the basic dimensions or varying the weight and the angle of the timber. The Helmholtz resonators are calibrated to the same set of dimensions.

With its allusion to the inn or the farmhouse parlor, this motif of "resonant paneling" serves as the only visual reference to the rural origins and the milieu of the music. However, with their cut-out shapes and the "breathing" proportions of their timber panels, the resonators shift this familiar motif from its trusted context, introducing it into a variable and unstable spatial atmosphere.

In other words, the basic spatial layout of the Klanghaus carries a certain allure. Starting from the chapel-like focus of a central hexagon, the "parlor" spirals outward, progressively relinquishing the certainty of a clear spatial typology—as a platform for music.

Fig. 1
Concert hall in Isfahan.

Fig. 2
Täferstube Muotatal.

Fig. 3
Introverted space in the Klanghaus.

8 **Entwurf: Der Klang der Räume – architektonisch** Der Verlockung der absoluten Offenheit unterliegt die Plattform nicht. Den vielschichtigsten und intensivsten Bezug zur Landschaft schafft eine Architektur, welche ein Gleichgewicht zwischen Öffnung und Intimität einhält. Die Räume bieten deshalb auch stille, introvertierte Momente an wie in einer Stube. Weil aber die wichtigen räumlichen Elemente beweglich sind, verändert sich der Charakter der Räume wie auf einer Bühne.

Konzertsaal Isfahan

Täferstube Muotatal

Klanghaus introvertierter Raum

Das Klanghaus ist ein reines Holzhaus. Es ist die Holzkonstruktion, welche die einfachste Einstellung der verschiedenen Resonanzen erlaubt und die feinste Abstufung zwischen Öffnung und Intimität von Räumen.

Herz des Hauses bildet ein in sich gekehrter, introvertierter Raum. Er verweist nicht nur auf die Konzentration der Musik, sondern paradoxerweise vor allem auf die Landschaft. Wie in der kleinen romanischen Kirche in den Bergen, sind es gerade die Ruhe und die Gefasstheit dieses Raums, welche die grandiose Weite der Landschaft gegenwärtig machen. Die Seitenarme, welche durch das Öffnen der Resonanz-Tore dazugeschaltet werden können, verändern die Raumwirkung vollkommen, das Haus wird nun Bühne. Die Seitenflügel sind fast wie Katapulte, die den Raum in die Landschaft schleudern.

Um die verschiedenen Raumzustände zusammenzuhalten, bilden die Wandoberflächen ein einheitliches Geflecht: die Holztäferung. Deren stark profilierte Oberfläche weist gute akustische Streueigenschaften auf. Die Möglichkeit, das Grundmass zu teilen oder zu vervielfachen sowie das Gewicht und den Anstellwinkel des Holzes zu variieren, bietet feine akustische Einstellungsmöglichkeiten. Die Helmhotz-Resonatoren unterwerfen sich derselben Massreihe.

Dieses Motiv der «klingenden Täferung» ist das einzige Motiv, das als Bild auch direkten Bezug nimmt auf die ländliche Herkunft der Musik und deren Milieu in den Anspielungen auf die Beiz oder die Bauernstube. Die Resonatoren mit ihren Schnittfiguren und die «atmenden» Proportionen der Holzfelder entführen das gewohnte Motiv aber weg vom Vertrauten in die Welt einer bewegten, instabilen Raumstimmung.

Es liegt also eine gewisse Verführung in der räumlichen Grundanordnung des Klanghauses. Ausgehend von der kapellenartigen Konzentration eines zentralen Hexagons entwickelt die «Stube» einen zunehmenden Zug gegen aussen und büsst dabei an der Gewissheit eines klaren Raumtyps ein – als Plattform für die Musik.

9 Design: The Sound of the Spaces—Musical

The Klanghaus is not a recording studio; rather, it is a volume that resonates and also admits sounds. It creates an unfamiliar yet soft and open acoustic atmosphere, permitting the musicians to "remain themselves," much like the yodeler outside the cowshed or the saxophonist in the club. The space is more tuned than cushioned or controlled. It displays a resonance that is broad and full and whose characteristics can be altered.

What are "ideal conditions for recording sound?" When is a space suitable for making music? And for making which form of music? The trend in sound engineering is to declare a certain acoustic environment as standard. The Klanghaus pursues another path. It aims to create architecture with a vibrant acoustic topography—a building that reflects sound in all its breadth and richness, offering a range of acoustic settings.

The musician should be able to play with and alter the acoustics. The building will not "solve acoustic problems" like a concert hall but, rather, contain complex, discoverable resonant environments. It will renounce the technically-driven intimidation of the recording studio. Playing here is more like participating in a project by Matthias Ziegler, who "performs" before Palladian villas or dam walls.

The centerpiece of these architectural acoustics is the "Isfahan" resonators: These dominate the spatial acoustics through their power and the images of instruments that are cut out of them as if by scissors. They can be tuned, opened, and closed, allowing medium and low pitches to be accentuated, broadened, or softened. The frequency range of the timber paneling tends to distribute the sound more broadly at the upper levels.

The teardrop-shaped space next to the practice room creates a large resonance chamber within the central volume. Above all, however, it is a specific place for music, much like every other space in the building. The same applies to the low reception space or the gallery to the dining room. This unpredictable "appropriation" of the spaces embodies the symbiosis between the authenticity of the music and an architecture that is at peace with itself. Musical curiosity opens up a building with an unmistakable acoustic fingerprint—much like a church.

"Controlled" acoustics will be found only in the northeast wing. These permit recordings to be made in studio conditions with the help of the production booth located on the gallery. However, there is no need for the cladding in this space to differ from that in the rest of the building, as the sound insulation ensures that recordings can take place undisturbed, even while courses are held at the same time.

Fig. 1
Paper-cut from Toggenburg.

Fig. 2
Section through the gallery and studio.

Fig. 3
Opening from the Klanghaus onto the landscape.

9 **Entwurf:**
Der Klang der Räume – musikalisch

Das Klanghaus ist kein Tonstudio, sondern ein Körper, der klingt und der auch Geräusche zulässt. Er schafft eine unbekannte, aber weiche, offene akustische Atmosphäre, welche dem Musiker erlaubt, «bei sich selbst zu bleiben» wie dem Jodler vor dem Stall – oder dem Saxofonisten im Club. Der Raum ist eher gestimmt als gedämpft oder «kontrolliert». Er weist eine breite, volle Resonanz auf, deren Charakteristika verändert werden.

Scherenschnitt Toggenburg

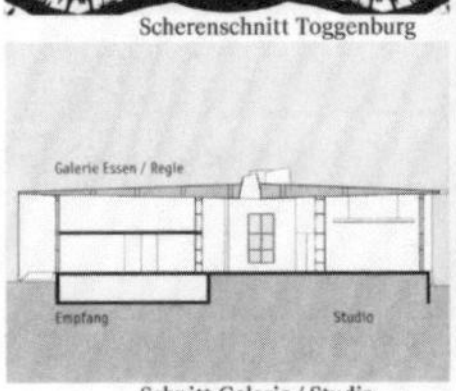

Schnitt Galerie / Studio

Klanghaus Öffnung hin zur Landschaft

Was sind «hervorragende Tonaufnahme-Bedingungen»? Wann eignet sich ein Raum für Musik? Und für welche? Akustik als Engineering neigt dazu, ein bestimmtes akustisches Klima zum Standard zu erklären.

Das Klanghaus verfolgt einen anderen Weg. Es will als Architektur eine aufregende akustische Topografie aufbauen, ein Haus, das Klänge in grosser Breite und Reichhaltigkeit reflektiert, das unterschiedliche akustische Orte schafft. Der Musiker soll mit der Akustik spielen können, diese verändern. Es werden nicht «akustische Probleme gelöst» wie in einem Konzertsaal, sondern komplexe Resonanzwelten eingerichtet, die sich aufspüren lassen. Es wird auf jede technische Einschüchterungsgebärde verzichtet, die Tonstudios eigen sind. Hier zu spielen, gleicht eher einem Projekt von Matthias Ziegler, der Palladio-Villen oder Staumauern «erspielt».

Im Zentrum dieses architektonischen Klangs stehen die «Isfahan»-Resonatoren: Sie beherrschen den Raum akustisch, durch ihre Wucht und durch die Instrumentenbilder, die wie Scherenschnitte ausgesägt sind. Sie sind stimmbar, lassen sich öffnen und schliessen, erlauben es, auch mittlere und tiefe Tonlagen hervorzuheben, sie breiter und weicher zu machen. Die Bandbreite in der Struktur des Holztäfers sorgt eher in oberen Bereichen für breite Klangverteilungen.

Die tropfenartige Kammer neben dem Übungsraum ist eine grosse Resonanzkammer des zentralen Raums. Aber vor allem ist sie ein eigener Ort für Musik, genau wie jeder andere Raum hier. Dies gilt auch für den niedrigen Empfangsraum oder für die Galerie des Essraums. In dieser unvorhersehbaren «Beschlagnahmung» der Räume begegnen sich die Authentizität der Musik und eine Architektur, die in sich selber ruht: Die musikalische Neugierde erschliesst sich ein Haus, das einen unverwechselbaren akustischen Fingerabdruck hat – genau wie eine Kirche.

Nur im Nordost-Flügel werden «kontrollierte» akustische Verhältnisse geschaffen. Sie erlauben, Aufnahmen unter Bedingungen eines Studios zu machen, und es gibt dafür auch einen Regieraum in der Galerie. Die Verkleidung dieser Räume braucht allerdings nicht anders zu sein als im übrigen Haus. Doch die Schallisolationen erlauben es, störungsfreie Aufnahmen oder parallele Kurse durchzuführen.

10 Epilogue: A Personal Postscript

This investigation became quite an odyssey. It became an unintended journey to the heart of traditional Swiss music. Numerous conversations with traditional—and experimental—musicians and a multitude of CDs and films transformed this research into an experience unlike any that I had previously had as an architect. What began as a clarification of a brief soon transformed into an ethnological immersion into a world I knew little about.

Over time, I became aware of the extent to which this culture is about much more than just music, and I gained a sense of a culture that is very much alive, although I had mistakenly assumed that it was fading away. I also saw how much of today's world has already penetrated this milieu, seemingly without resistance. And I began to understand why the music had changed so little. For example, the more I listened to yodeling, the more I appreciated its determination to defend its own identity. As Hans-Jürg Sommer's "Moosruef" echoed in my ear, I grasped why certain forms of music are slow to evolve and so selective about what they integrate from other traditions. But a dozen exceptional specialists on the Alpine horn under the direction of an empathic jazz player were enough to coax a stunning new sound from the "Ruef." This cautious approach to everything that merges with everything else often resonates with me in the art world as well. But then I have also been fascinated by the eccentrics from Valais or Central Switzerland who showcase their unique expressions so shamelessly at the margins.

It has always been personal encounters that have changed my perspective: with the elderly lead yodeler in Muotatal, who sang me the "natural F" in his kitchen, with the extraordinary büchel player in the same valley, and with the virtuoso on the Swiss hand organ in Toggenburg who introduced me to his jazz collection.

Without such experiences, the project might have resulted in a consummate building, but nothing more. However, I wanted to answer the deeper question of how architecture and music can truly come together. My immersion in this proud culture taught me two things, amongst others: First, only an architecture that is certain of its own principles speaks meaningfully to music. And second, there really are invisible lines, where this convergence becomes compelling.

MM, March 2010

Fig. 1
Towards the lake.

Fig. 2
Towards the valley.

Fig. 3
The axes in the topography.

10 **Epilog**
Eine persönliche Nachbemerkung

Für diese Untersuchung bin ich ziemlich weit herumgekommen. Sie geriet zu einer Reise ins Innere der Schweizer Volksmusik, die so nicht geplant war. Zahlreiche Gespräche mit Volksmusikern, auch mit experimentellen Musikern, eine Menge CD und Filme haben diese Recherche zu etwas gemacht, womit ich als Architekt noch nie zu tun hatte. Das war keine «Programmabklärung», sondern eine ethnologische Erfahrung in einer mir kaum bekannten Welt.

Mit der Zeit wurde mir klar, wie weit diese Kultur über die Musik hinausreicht, weil sie einem wachen Lebensgefühl Ton gibt, von dem ich annahm, dass es am Verglimmen sei. Aber ich habe auch gesehen, wie viel Gegenwart in diese Lebenswelt schon eingedrungen ist, scheinbar ohne Schmerzen. Und ich begann zu ahnen, warum sich in dieser Musik nur wenig bewegt. Je mehr ich zugehört habe, desto mehr hat etwa der Jodel meine Sympathie gefunden, wenn er seine Grenzen hütet. Mit Hans-Jürg Sommers «Moosruef» im Ohr ist mir begreiflich geworden, warum sich eine Musik nur zögernd verändert, und sich eben nicht mit allem anderen «crosst»: Ein Dutzend herausragende Alphornspezialisten unter der Leitung eines empathischen Jazzers haben ausgereicht, um dem „Ruef" einen neuen, umwerfenden Klang abzugewinnen. Diese Zurückhaltung gegenüber allem, was sich mit allem anderen mischt, beschleicht mich in der Kunst oft. Aber dann habe ich auch fasziniert jenen schrägen Vögeln aus dem Wallis oder der Innerschweiz zugehört, die so schamlos auf den Rändern herumtanzen.

Immer waren es persönliche Begegnungen, die meine Sicht verändert haben: mit dem alten Vorjodler im Muotatal, der mir in der Küche das Natur-Fa vorgesungen hat, mit dem unglaublichen Büchelsolo im selben Tal, mit dem Meister des Schwyzerörgeli im Toggenburg, der mich in seine Jazz-Sammlung eingeführt hat.

Ohne solche Erlebnisse wäre das Projekt vielleicht eine virtuose Architektur geworden, mehr nicht. Aber ich wollte eine Antwort finden auf die Frage, wie sich Architektur und Musik überhaupt begegnen können. Der Einblick in eine stolze Kultur hat mich zwei Dinge gelehrt, unter anderem: Nur eine Architektur, die sich ihrer eigenen Regeln sicher ist, hat der Musik überhaupt etwas zu sagen; und: Es gibt tatsächlich verborgene Linien, wo die Begegnung aufregend wird.

MM, März 2010

Zum See hin

Zum Talraum hin

Die Achsen in der Topografie

Approaching Sound. Conversations with Sound Artist Andres Bosshard and Acoustician Martin Lachmann

Sabine von Fischer

Listening, humming, thinking, I approach the Klanghaus taking the detour of the Klangweg (Sound Trail) that is in some sense not a detour at all: it is these paths that enable us to understand the building of the Klanghaus, which is a spatial score, composed from the sounds of the landscape. The acoustician Martin Lachmann will explain to me later, in our conversation, that it is a hybrid of space and instrument, and sound artist Andres Bosshard will initiate a dialogue between body and space. It is these experiences for which the detours to this special building are preparing me.

A paved road leads directly from Iltios, the intermediate station on the funicular, to the building. But it is worth deviating via the higher Klangweg, one of the many paths through the landscape between Schwendisee and Chäserrugg. All along this Klangweg, one hears sounds from near and far, and there are special listening places, installations with musical instruments, a multitude of familiar and surprising sounds. A telephone box asks for my auditory impressions. The powerlines buzz in the summer sky.

The mental, emotional, physiological preparation for the Klanghaus is achieved through a series of experiences: the crunch of gravel under our feet, the distant rock faces, the colorful flowers, several wooden or metallic instruments, the rustling of leaves in the wind, the platforms for listeners, the twitter of birds, the drone of planes, the singing of the ropeway masts and much more.

In the niche of the entrance on the north side, I chat with Bosshard, the sound artist from Zurich, who also describes himself as a “gardener of sound” and helped to shape the ideas for the Klanghaus. We listen to the echo from the rock formations on the other side of the valley and to the sound of car engines. I sit with Lachmann on the terrace below the overhanging canopy, as the resin drips from the freshly-sawn wooden shingles. He is an acoustician who

Fig. 1

Fig. 1
Tuning of the spaces with the sound artist Andres Bosshard and acoustician Martin Lachmann, autumn 2024.

addresses singular problems, the founder of the company Applied Acoustics, and was involved in the design of this special building from day one.

It smells of wood, outside and in. The wind carries our voices to the meadows and across the small lake. Inside the Klanghaus' central space, thin bronze mirrors and heavy wooden panels send the tones across and through the space. Sounds are moving in all directions.

Anyone who comes to the Klanghaus moves, too: on their feet, walking, in their ears, listening, and in their head, thinking. When we speak, sound waves oscillate through the air; the building and the landscape join in: words, ideas, memories reverberate.

Sabine von Fischer in conversation with Andres Bosshard, July 2024

Andreas Bosshard, is the Klanghaus your biggest work?

> It's certainly the biggest in terms of its importance. In terms of scale, it's more of a medium-sized project; it is, after all, a building for people. This is neither a tower nor an arena but rather, a place that is to be inhabited. The human voice—speaking and singing—is the starting point.

When I enter, the size of the building surprises me.

> The spatial volume was determined by the initial idea of a triangle spanning between three trees. People stand within these tree trunks while the crowns of the trees spread above them. The three curves in the walls of the central space are the traces of these imagined trees. On the outside, they form parabolas that face the landscape. On the inside, this central space is the belly of the building, where the three concave, inwardly curving elements of wall, together with the doors to the outside, recall the idea of the

tree trunks. We don't step outside from a space—we step outside from a place.

And this place is based on the human scale?

Yes, but not only. The sound paths have different radii. Inside the building they're small or medium-sized, but out here they're almost endless. Säntis is seven kilometers away, and the wall in front of which we're sitting refers to this space. When thunder rings out, the building captures it with this parabolically curved facade. Do you hear that car driving past? The sound comes from behind and back from above, and the building answers. Christian Zehnder, Artistic Director of the Klangwelt, recently put it really well: "When I sing, then the building answers me. There's a dialogue."

How does this dialogue come about?

The space isn't just a vessel that returns the sound. It's also a persona, a figure. It not only returns the sound, but also speaks with it. In the interior, it does this thanks to the bronze acoustic mirrors in the central space.

And nature joins in this dialogue.

We used these acoustic mirrors to draw the landscape into the building: on that rock face over there and this one and this one, are different mirrors of different sizes in very specific positions. Christian recently sent a gift my way by saying: "The sound from those mirrors is like a natural echo, but in their natural setting, I can never hear them to the very end, since there are always other sounds out there. Inside this building, I can finally hear the natural echo right to the end."

So the building works at many scales, from that of the human being to that of a rock face.

The wavelengths that we can hear range from around seventeen millimeters to seventeen meters, which corresponds to approximately twenty kilohertz to twenty hertz. Up to around 2.2 meters, I'm speaking of the actual dimensions of the human body, whereas seventeen meters refers to a very large body that we can't even envisage. We composed the architectural requirements of the sounds in such a way that the body and the space can speak to each other.

How does this differ from a classic concert hall?

There's no front or rear; everything is all around us. There isn't just left and right: we can also hear very clearly behind our heads. We start with our own body. This is an acoustic body that the musicians can activate—with which they can play.

How do you play with the acoustic space?

When I play music, I set myself two fundamental tasks. The first is that the music should move within the space. The basic movement is a vibration, a rotation of the sound in the space. The second task is that the tone should move upwards. I thoroughly tested this in the Klangturm (Sound Tower) at the Expo.02 in Biel. The sound also floats in the same way in the central space here. And this floating is perceived as a sort of spatial rotation.

It seems impossible to situate the sounds in the central space. They're ringing everywhere.

That's how we composed it. We spent a long time testing the positions of the mirrors: a continuous row of small acoustic mirrors at body height and larger ones higher up. The large bronze mirrors resonate for longer, which allows the dying echo to rise within the space. I discussed this with Marcel Meili at length: we're making an instrument that's waiting for someone to interact with it. Everyone should do what they want. This wonderfully fine echo in the walls of the central space is the secret of the Klanghaus.

You said that, in terms of your complete oeuvre, the Klanghaus is a medium-sized project. Which were your smallest and your largest works?

The largest is *Echoes from the Moon*, which I was able to make with Pauline Oliveros in Salzburg in 1997. She was not only one of the most important composers of electronic music, but also a feminist, and she said that space travel is only ever about men. So she wanted to send her voice to the moon and listen back to it. This "Space Opera" was created in response to the invitation to contribute to the Golden Record on *Voyager II*. We performed the piece twice, in Salzburg and in St. Pölten for the opening of the Klangturm. Anyone could shout "hello," and the loudspeaker played back the radiophone echo from the surface of the moon. The wonderful thing was that this is most effective in silence. The louder it is, the less one hears the space.

And the smallest work?

The smallest work of all featured the Klangwürfel (Sound Cubes) that Aya Masui and I made for Harald Naegeli in Zurich in 2021. We created lots of small—or even tiny—cube-shaped loudspeakers for the visitors to the Musée Visionnaire, where his *Wolkenbilder* were on show. Aya had designed a performance with micro sounds, in which the gentle rustling of paper built up in the loudspeakers for an hour until it became a sort of distant thunderstorm. Naegeli's paintings are a similar, infinitely delicate tissue of woven lines. It was as if the audience was left floating weightlessly in both space and time.

Does this tiny dimension recur in the Klanghaus?

There's this statement by Michel Chion, who's also written lots about sounds and *Musique concrète*: he says that we never take the time to let a sound fully die away. Music from a grand piano requires sixteen seconds. No piece of music makes full use of this time. This approach to listening takes us from music to another sort of listening. These notions of listening into, listening within, and staying with the sounds as they fade away are also essential to the Klanghaus.

Sabine von Fischer
in conversation with
Martin Lachmann, July 2024

Martin Lachmann, you work just as much with musicians as with architects. When they talk about auditory spaces, do they all understand the same thing?

Amongst the artists, the musicians, I'm pretty sure they do. I became familiar with their way of describing and talking about sound in the early years of my career as a sound engineer. The way we're talking now, here in the Klanghaus, about how it will sound in the future, is just like the way one discusses the intentions for the sounds before a recording session.

And in architecture?

There, this discussion about the auditory experience is less common, but there are exceptions, such as Marcel Meili. We debated exhaustively during the competition phase and realized that there's no standard performance space for traditional music. In classical music, for example, the format of a hall for chamber music is relatively clearly defined and spaces are built for a specific orchestral setup or size of audience.

Fig. 2
Listening to sound generated by a digital model of the Klanghaus in the studio, with, amongst others, Dominik Kessler, Martin Lachmann, Edi Hartmann (Cultural Office, St.Gallen, now Klangwelt). Far right Marcel Meili, photographed by Astrid Staufer, 2013.

Fig. 2

In contrast, traditional music is played both inside and outside.

And not just that, the spectrum is incredibly wide: The places where people play traditional music range from the "parlor" of a farmhouse, where the "Stubete" (parlor concert) takes place, via the school gym or multipurpose hall to the festival tent. Or in the open air. These very different spaces were the starting point for our conceptualization of the Klanghaus. We realized that there's no standard performance space for natural or acoustic music—for "traditional music" in the widest sense.

The curved facades of the Klanghaus embrace the landscape: Are these external areas also performance spaces?

Yes—hence the form. These are performance spaces out here, just as the shell-shaped bandstand in the spa gardens is a performance space for the orchestra. And the acoustic intention is the same: there's a wall behind the musicians and, above this, a ceiling that projects the sound outwards. Here, the Klanghaus works in two ways: On the one hand it's a parabolic mirror. If I stand here at the focal point, I can hear the sounds of the landscape even more intensely. On the other hand, these walls also project sounds outwards.

Upon entering the central space of the Klanghaus, the senses are inundated—optically and acoustically. What's the intention here?

It's particularly interesting that the rich decoration of this building is more than just an acoustic requirement. It has much more to do with Meili's design and his references, such as kaleidoscopic foliage or the perforated surfaces of Isfahan that inspired the resonators in the walls. For me as an acoustician, this is a rare occasion on which I haven't had to argue against smooth surfaces. These diverse structures all accompanied the design idea. We then calculated the acoustic characteristics on the basis of these ideas—using both computer models and mathematical-analytical methods. This enabled us to make use of our experience with other special spatial challenges, such as the black organ hall for the Toni Campus at ZHdK, where we achieved an extremely diffuse sound field with the help of convex wall surfaces. We were effectively able to trick the space into seeming larger to the listener.

How does the size of a space inform the design process?

The greater the spatial volume, the greater the range of acoustic possibilities. This is why we also used elements in the Klanghaus, such as the acoustic mirrors in the central space, that make it seem larger, as a means of leveraging the physical limits of the restricted built volume. We had no reference projects because there has never been such a building. Here, everything was possible and nothing was predefined. But this also required lots of work and we produced an unbelievable quantity of calculations and computer simulations. And, at the end of the day, the building produces rather extraordinary sounds.

You generally reject the popular notion that "a music room is like an instrument." Do you make an exception here?

In principle, I stand by my criticism. In the usual case of buildings, the suggestion that the space is an instrument is simply not valid—it's incomplete and oversimplified. But I have to qualify this criticism in the case of the central space of the Klanghaus: this space has an active component. An acoustic space is usually completely different from an instrument: it has no active component and only reverberates when an instrument is played and stimulates the volume. The space is not the instrument. The central space with its distinctively active component is different. In this sense it's a hybrid and the distinction between space and instrument becomes blurred.

Andres Bosshard calls it a dialogue between the space and the spatial response.

Every space responds; these responses are everywhere. Even the silence of a completely soundproof room can be described as a spatial response—not saying anything says a lot. In a church with a lengthy echo, every layperson is aware of this acoustic response.

How would you describe the spatial response of the Klanghaus?

Thanks to the ideas of Meili and Bosshard, we designed a hybrid active space. The Klanghaus becomes active using the resources of the space itself, and not the electronic resources to which the term "active" usually refers in the vocabulary of acousticians. This approach enabled us to outsmart the limited spatial volume and make it seem larger with the help of purely passive measures. The acoustic mirrors resonate powerfully and, like all other surfaces, are also activated by the sounds in the space. However, due to their structure, these acoustic mirrors resonate far longer and it's this that creates the impression of a much larger spatial volume. The idea worked far better than I expected, because they produce a surprisingly natural spatial response—which is much longer than such a building could produce alone.

Do these powerful acoustic characteristics of the central space at Toggenburg mean that works should be specially composed for this space and, if so, what types of works?

I would certainly support this. The central space is an experimental space, per se—triggering in us the desire to carry out our own experiments. A wide range is possible here—definitely including acoustic music. The space is hardly suitable for pop or rock. I can imagine a lot of jazz, music from the entire classical spectrum, and, especially, music from the original area of the Klanghaus, traditional music with its natural singing voices and traditional instruments—in other words, acoustic music in the broadest sense.

Holes in the Wall. Ali Qapu and the Klanghaus

Axel Langer

3,900 kilometers from Wildhaus, as the crow flies, is the city of Isfahan, the capital of the Persian Safavid Empire, which was built by Shah Abbas I (who ruled from 1587 to 1626). At the time, several of the city's opulent new structures were already being used by princes and architects in both East and West as models for projects such as the Avenue des Champs-Elysées in Paris, which can be traced back to Chahar Bagh, Isfahan's garden boulevard. In turn, the niche-filled walls of the domed hall of Ali Qapu inspired a series of spaces in Indian palaces between the seventeenth and the nineteenth centuries.[1] 400 years later, Marcel Meili oriented his design for the central space in the Klanghaus on the "Music Hall" of Ali Qapu.[2]

Prelude

A fleeting comparison confirms the formal correspondence between the two spaces: the central design elements are the perforated walls. The acoustic holes in both spaces have the form of objects, either vessels as in Isfahan, or musical instruments as in the original design by Meili. The similarities continue on the acoustic level, as we will see below. In both Isfahan and Wildhaus, the surfaces and recesses in the walls act as Helmholtz resonators. However, the acousticians in Wildhaus took a different approach by also building in singing bowls—elements that are not found in Isfahan.

One could imagine that there is nothing more to be said. But this is not quite true, because an apparently secondary question remains open: What are the silhouettes of these resonators all about?

Exposition

Let us start by turning to Ali Qapu in Isfahan. The name signifies "Lofty Gateway," and the structure marks the threshold between the huge Shah Square and the palace

1 Mehreen Chida-Razvi, "From Function to Form: Chini-khana in Safavid and Mughal Architecture," in *South Asian Studies*, 2019, vol. 35, no. 1, pp. 82–106; Esther Schmidt "Negotiating Cosmopolitan Taste with Local Culture: Porcelain Rooms in Indian Forts and Palaces," in John Stobart (ed.), *Global Goods and Country House: Comparative Perspectives, 1650–1800*, London, 2023, pp. 307–330.

2 Marcel Meili, "Neun Thesen und eine persönliche Nachbemerkung zum Entwurf für das Klanghaus Toggenburg," in Hochbauamt des Kantons St.Gallen, Amt für Kultur, Kanton St.Gallen, *Klanghaus Toggenburg. Thesenkonkurrenz/Thesis Competition. Bericht des Preisgerichts/Report of the Jury*, 2010, proposition 8, p. 32, here p. 25.

Fig. 1

Fig. 2

Fig. 1
The decoration of the sound holes as foreseen in the thesis competition for the central space of the Klanghaus. Marcel Meili, *Thesis Competition*, 2010.

Fig. 2
Domed hall in Ali Qapu Palace in Isfahan. A reference for the Klanghaus.

Fig. 3

Fig. 4

Fig. 5

Fig. 6

Fig. 3
Theorbo, Sebastian Schelle, Nuremberg, 1728.

Fig. 4
Drawing of the sound hole of the theorbo (fig. 3).

Fig. 5
Frontispiece of a *Masnavi* manuscript for Sultan Walad, Egypt, 1366, Folio 77b.

Fig. 6
Central rosette (detail from fig. 5). The sound holes of string instruments were crafted according to the same principles in Europe for many years. The circular opening is generally filled with a form of lattice structure. Astonishing parallels are often found with the book art of the Islamic World. The most important examples include the illuminated frontispieces of lavish manuscripts, the centers of which contain a so-called *shamseh* or "sun" medallion. In the case of the Egyptian *Masnavi* manuscript this is a form of quatrefoil motif that is created by interweaving two strands of forked leaves. The same idea of combining several decorative motifs arranged in circles is found in the sound holes of the theorboes. The basic forms are also similar.

complex. However, this gateway is more than just a place of transition: The individual levels, read from bottom to top, faithfully represent the "imperial machinery."[3] This ends on the fifth level in the above-mentioned domed hall, which was created around 1615.

Although this space is generally known as the "Music Hall," we are less sure of its function than this description would lead us to suspect—even if much points in this direction. When the building was comprehensively renovated in the 1970s, initial experiments with Iranian musicians confirmed the extraordinary acoustics of the domed hall, with its perforated gypsum panels.[4] In 2008, Hassan Azad from Tehran University used a computer simulation[5] to confirm the fact that, thanks to the openings in the *muqarnas* or stalactite vaulting,[6] the space truly does have outstanding properties. Azad states that, despite its height, the space is ideally suited to the recitation of poetry and the performance of classic Persian music with its small ensembles.

Conversely, the interrelated questions of the function of the niches in the walls and why the incised silhouettes resemble vessels have still not been unequivocally answered today.

The niche-filled walls in Ali Qapu are closely related to those of Chini Khaneh, the "House of Porcelain," of the shrine in Ardabil, which was built in 1611. Chini Khaneh is home to 1,126 pieces of Chinese blue-and-white porcelain, a sizeable royal collection that was transferred by Shah Abbas to Ardabil as a *waqf* or charitable endowment.[7] Here, the niches served as display cases, in which vases, plates, bottles, ewers and other containers were exhibited as in a museum. This created a formal relationship between these niches, whose silhouettes invoke a range of ceramic vessels, and the containers that were actually on display.[8] However, there are serious doubts as to whether this was also the case in the domed hall of Ali Qapu.[9]

But if it was not planned to exhibit porcelain here, why do these silhouettes refer to vessels?

Development

A possible answer is offered by Persian wall paintings of the same period, which must originally have also decorated the dado of the domed hall.[10] Valuable golden or ceramic vessels—which also included Chinese porcelain—were a regular feature of the depictions of loving couples, amorous picnic scenes and graceful servants. A notable role was played by the long-necked bottle, from which young women and men served each other wine. These young people are cupbearers (Persian: *saqi*). In Persia's mystically inspired poetry, a *saqi* (Persian grammar makes no distinction between the genders), can be a dispenser of drink or a lover,

3 Sussan Babaie, *Isfahan and Its Palaces: Statecraft, Shi'ism and the Architecture of Conviviality in Early Modern Iran*, Edinburgh, 2008, p. 149.

4 Eugenio Galdieri, *Esfahan: Ali Qapu: An Architectural Survey*, Rome, 1979, p. 21.

5 Hassen Azad, "Ali Qapu: Persian Historical Music Room," in *akuTEK, Proceedings of the Institute of Acoustics*, vol. 30, part 3, 2008 (https://www.akutek.info/Papers/HA_Persian.pdf), see, in particular, Fig. 5.

6 In reality, the vaults are not loadbearing but, much more, a form of huge plaster shell that, as suggested by the original Arab term, hangs down from the ceiling; in Ali Qapu, these are attached to hemp ropes, which are coated with plaster (Galdieri 1979, p. 63).

7 The origins of Chini Khaneh can be traced back to the fifteenth century, although no architectural evidence of this remains. In his memoirs, Babur mentions the House of Porcelain that his ancestor Ulugh Beg (who ruled from 1447 to 1449) had had built (Schmidt 2023, p. 308). See also Linda Komaroff, "Chinese Porcelains from the Ardabil Shrine: Collecting and Display in Iran," in Ali M. Ansari and Melanie Gibson (eds.), *Fruit of Knowledge, Wheel of Learning: Essays in Honour of Carole and Robert Hillenbrand*, London, 2022, vol. 2, pp. 268–85.

8 Chinese porcelain was also exhibited in special rooms in Europe. A good example of this is a cabinet in the "Retirade" of the Duchess in Schloss Friedenstein in Gotha. Here, the wall was fitted with brackets, on which valuable vessels were presented.

9 Chida-Razvi 2019, pp. 86–87. Many of the wall niches are only suitable for presentation to a limited extent due to the form of their openings.

10 Galdieri 1979, p. 21 and the note in footnote 1.

but the term can also allude to God. Wine, on the other hand, represents the sacred light (the knowledge) that is poured into the wine glass (the heart of the mystic). The *saqi* is also linked to the *Saqinameh*, the "The Book of the Cupbearer," a literary genre that was particularly flourishing in the seventeenth century. And *Saqinameh* also signifies a specific sequence of musical notes that is used as a basis for improvisation.[11]

This brings us back full circle to the "Music Hall." These brief remarks, which relate to the silhouettes of vessels, thus refer visually to music, poetry, and wine; they are figurative allusions to Sufi inspiration. In other words, the space provides a retreat from everyday life and, on a higher level, a place of rapture.

It is not without reason that this interpretation recalls an illumination in a sixteenth-century manuscript, which is read as an "Allegory of Worldly and Otherworldly Drunkenness." This shows the great mystic poet Hafiz on the uppermost level of a tavern[12] and, above him on the roof and below the open sky, solemnizing angels. On the top level of Ali Qapu, this reference is architecturally confirmed by the dome, whose golden *muqarnas* vault resembles a heavenly canopy that spans above the rectangular floor plan. Facing the Lofty Gateway on the opposite side of the large square is the Sheikh Lotfollah Mosque, whose dome is no less impressive and whose construction probably started around 1611/12. Given the range of symbolic references that connect the individual buildings on Isfahan's main square, it seems obvious that the domed hall of Ali Qapu is intended to act as a mystic counterpart to the religious domed space of the mosque.

Recapitulation

Let us now turn to the central space in Wildhaus. In an earlier phase of the project, its wooden paneled walls, which recall those of a farmhouse parlor,[13] were decorated with openings, whose outlines invoked instruments such as horns or cellos. As the design process advanced, the rigidly rectangular layout of the panels gave way to a more rhythmic, more musical organization.[14] And rather than instruments, the silhouettes now recall sound holes, such as those that are typically found on a dulcimer, the epitome of music in Toggenburg. In this way, the opening in the form of a sound hole no longer refers to the instrument that generates the sound, but rather, to the place in which that sound rings out, and hence, to the sound itself. The purely formal relationship between the silhouette and the spatial function (as was also determined at Chini Khaneh) has been replaced by a relationship that hints at a higher meaning. The wall itself becomes an instrument, an acoustic body, and the space in front of it the actual acoustic volume. Thus, the architects have achieved the same focus

11 Thomas Ogger, "Hafiz und Goethe, ihre Sprache und Musik," in *Spektrum Iran*, 26th yr., no. 4, 2013, pp. 98ff.

12 Hafiz (who died in 1390) is not only one of the greatest Persian poets but also often sings of the *saqi* in his ghazals.

13 Meili 2010, proposition 8, p. 32, here p. 25.

14 The wall openings now look like different voices positioned above each other in a score.

Fig. 7

Fig. 8

Fig. 9

Fig. 10

Fig. 7
Chini Khaneh, interior, Ardabil.

Fig. 8
Illumination from a *Divan* of Hafiz, Sultan Mohammad, 1530/31.

Fig. 9
View into the dome of Ali Qapu.

Fig. 10
Acoustic representation of the resonance wall with overdimensioned openings from hammered dulcimers in the central space of the Klanghaus, construction project, 2013.

①
8 mm plywood panels ($8\ kg/m^2$) with 20 cm cavity and 10 cm insulation ($30\ kg/m^3$).

②
20 mm perforated plywood panel directly supported by 42 mm three-layer panel ($20\ kg/m^2$), 50 cm total cavity, 10 cm insulation ($30\ kg/m^3$) fixed to rear surface.

③
20 mm perforated plywood panel directly supported by 35 mm insulation ($50\ kg/m^3$), 55 cm total cavity, 10 cm insulation ($50\ kg/m^3$) fixed to rear surface.

④
20 mm heavily perforated plywood panel, 55 cm cavity with acoustic mirrors made from bronze sheet and with diameters ranging from 90 to 220 cm.

⑤
20 mm heavily perforated plywood panel, 55 cm cavity.

⑥
20 mm heavily perforated plywood panel directly supported by 42 mm three-layer panel ($20\ kg/m^2$), 50 cm total cavity, 10 cm insulation ($30\ kg/m^3$) fixed to rear surface.

⑦
Door leaf made from two layers of 20 mm perforated plywood panel.

Fig. 11

Fig. 12

Fig. 13

Fig. 14

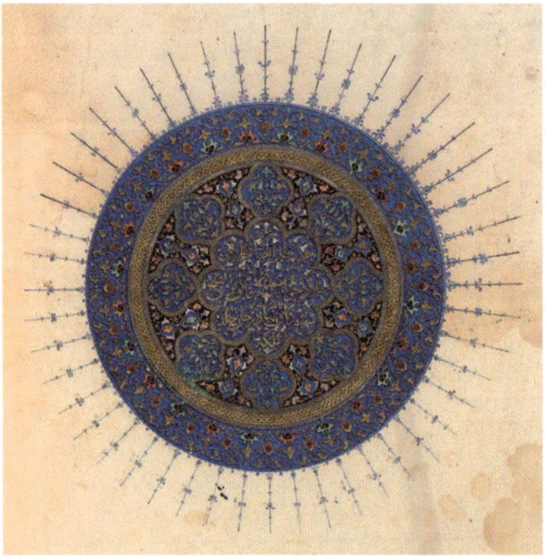

Fig. 15

Fig. 11
Hammered dulcimer, Germany, around 1608.

Fig. 12
Water filter, Egypt, probably thirteenth or fourteenth century.

Fig. 13
View into the domed ceiling of the music room of Ali Qapu (detail). Alongside examples from Islamic book art, further parallels include those between the earthen water filter with its pointed star and the sound holes of a German Renaissance hammered dulcimer. In both cases, the arms of the star are grooved. It is a short step to the *muqarna* vault of Ali Qapu.

Fig. 14
Hammered dulcimer, Joachim Muntz, Fronberg, 1757.

Fig. 15
Frontispiece of a *Masnavi* manuscript, Iran, sixteenth century. The formal similarities revealed by these comparative examples from Europe and the Islamic World are less astonishing than one may initially assume. This is explained by the fact that this ornamentation is based on the principles of practical geometry. In both cases, the artisans worked with a compass and a straight edge.

on the essential as in the domed hall of Ali Qapu. And, just as Isfahan's domed hall becomes the embodiment of mystically inspired pleasure, the space in Toggenburg becomes a "place for free musical work,"[15] which concentrates on the quality of the space itself. One space emphasizes the reception of the sound and the other its production.

15 Meili 2010, proposition 2, p. 25, here p. 19.

Finale

In both cases, and this is an unexpected insight, it is eventually the ornamentation that, in addition to its acoustic function, becomes the visible expression of the essence of the space itself. This ornamentation is not just decoration; it is a bearer of meaning. In this respect, the architects of the Klanghaus and those of Ali Qapu are even closer to each other than was suggested by the purely visual comparison at the beginning of this article.

A Built Resonator. Discovering Space, Sound, and Structure

Eva Kuss

Marcel Meili's nine propositions provide the conceptual framework for the Klanghaus ⊖. By combining precision with openness, this framework enabled the architecture to emerge, to become richer and find a concrete form. Everything seems so simple, and yet these propositions led, as if axiomatically, to a highly differentiated and very special building. Anyone who is familiar with design processes will be aware how unusual this is: a planning process that begins with a big "idea" can rapidly become banal. The fact that this did not happen here is partly due to the skill and broad experience of Marcel Meili and to his profound preparatory discussions with the musician and intendant Peter Roth and experts such as the sound artist Andres Bosshard and the timber building specialist Hermann Blumer. But it is also clearly due to his method of appropriating the design in a way that is simultaneously abstract and concrete—of finding a form, certainly, but without thinking formally.

⊖ Contribution by Marcel Meili, p. 18

In addition to this, the unique nature of the building task and the special local situation also contributed to the convincing outcome. The death of Marcel Meili during the development of the project ⊖ and the decision to realize it on the basis of a cooperative tender process led initially to an intense dialogue between the participating planners and, subsequently, to an early constructive exchange between these planners and the builders. Despite the predetermined cost constraints, they worked closely together to find solutions that would be capable of transforming the propositions for the Klanghaus into reality. This led to a process in which all the participants—all the local or regional companies and craftspeople who had teamed up cooperatively to form consortia—developed an artisanal discourse in which they increasingly identified with the building.

⊖ Contribution by Andrea Wiegelmann, p. 70

"The Klanghaus is a spatial and acoustic installation, whose meaning is not immediately apparent. It has to be discovered like an objet trouvé."[1]

1 Marcel Meili, "Neun Thesen und eine persönliche Nachbemerkung zum Entwurf für das Klanghaus Toggenburg," in Hochbauamt des Kantons St.Gallen, Amt für Kultur, Kanton St.Gallen, *Klanghaus Toggenburg. Thesenkonkurrenz/Thesis Competition. Bericht des Preisgerichts/Report of the Jury*, 2010, proposition 7, p. 31, here p. 24.

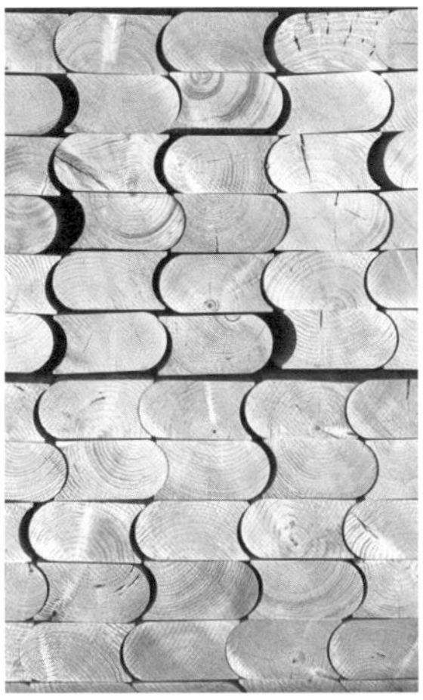

Fig. 1

Fig. 2

Fig. 1
End view of the six-centimeter-thick, knuckle-jointed solid timber blocks with milled joints, before they are assembled to form curved elements of wall.

Fig. 2
S-shaped gutter support destined for the edge of the roof above the loggia. It consists of two curved laminated timber elements with an inclined milled finish and an insulated gutter tray, prior to being lined with EPDM sheeting.

Discoveries

The central theme of this architecture is sound. As with the resonator of an instrument, it is the consideration of sound that determines the forms of the building as well as the choice of materials and the detailed design: "Toggenburg is a valley of wooden instruments rather than of brass instruments."[2] The building should also sound like a wooden instrument. And timber building is also the traditional construction method in the valley: wooden shingles and windows shape the appearance of the historical and now, once again, contemporary residential and agricultural buildings. However, while this selection of a material used in instrument-making and the local building tradition was self-evident, the full-scale implementation of the curved forms that would be able to produce the desired sound was extremely challenging. Timber buildings are inherently created by joining together linear elements using an orthogonal constructional logic. In structural terms, the Klanghaus now consists of curved blocks of stud wall, whose individual elements are interconnected using knuckle joints—a constructional innovation that was developed in a dialogue between the designers and the timber builders. These curved walls are now capped by an arched roof structure that owes its acoustic impact to its overhanging coved eaves. As in the (resonating) body of a violin, this roof sits on the walls, supporting a cylindrical crown that contains openings for both daylight and ventilation. By rising towards the center in this way, this solution combines structural optimization with the function of draining water from the roof.

Upon approaching the Klanghaus, we are initially surprised by its indeterminate scale. The building regularly opens up and closes without any sense of recognizable hierarchy. Despite its atypically curved external walls and expressively arched roof, it sits calmly in and merges with the landscape.

2 Hermann Blumer in the group dialogue about the building on July 12, 2024.

Fig. 3

Fig. 4

Fig. 5

Fig. 6

Fig. 7

Fig. 8

Fig. 3
The "Alte Rathaus" in Tufertschwil, a post-and-plank timber-framed house from 1654 with a mantle of red ochre—a red earth—with a high level of iron oxide. The term Rathaus has a colloquial ambiguity and, by blending the words Rot (red), Rat (council), and Rhode (a subdivision of a village), indicates not only color and social significance but also the definition of boundaries.

Fig. 4
Farmhouse in Lüpfertwil near Ebnat-Kappel with the rows of whitewashed windows that are typical for the cultural area set in a facade of charred timber cladding.

Fig. 5
View of the wall cladding in the Iltios music room with the three acoustic horizons made from solid beech slats and beech plywood.

Fig. 6
The stained oak slats sweep rhythmically upwards, setting the steps to music as they climb to the upper floor or descend to the basement. These are surrounded by fiberboard paneling with negative joints—red surfaces with white edges and, behind, dark shadows that emphasize the sense of rotation.

Fig. 7
The central space showing the view towards the Schwendisee music room when the "Isfahan doors" are closed. The doors in the external walls that curve inwards offer views towards the external stages.

Fig. 8
The central space, with a view towards the Schwendisee music room when the "Isfahan doors" are open. To the right, a pocket of space is visible—the echo room.

It seems to have been here forever.

It is only after passing the street-facing prow below the arched canopy and catching a view of the central space through the large opening that we discover the entrance hidden in a sort of gap. Thus, we arrive by walking a loop, turning in to this special structure and its musicality as if we are following a dance step. We then enter the building via the striking entrance door, behind which a double-height lobby rises vertically before opening out into an organically shaped stair hall. It is here that we first encounter the motif of the wall panel, paneling that accompanies our journey through the building in a multitude of variations. The cladding of internal walls with wooden panels is a typical approach for not only the farmhouse parlors of the region but also reception rooms in general. In the generously dimensioned Klangräume (Sound Spaces) of the Klanghaus, this wall paneling offers the intimacy of the parlor. And while it primarily serves to create a rich sound and control the acoustics, it is also a motif that directly highlights the rural associations of the music ➲. Its design and detailing vary from space to space, contributing to their individual characters as well as to the overall acoustic effect.

➲ Contribution by Lea Hagmann, Sonja Lieberherr-Schnyder, p. 94

The motif is applied in its most abstract, almost inverse form in the stair hall: the fiberboard panels prescribed by the fire regulations are mounted with varyingly spaced negative joints as a means of underlining the functional difference between the stair hall and the Klangräume. Here, in this transition zone between the outside world and the interior spaces, the colors of the Klanghaus are at their most intense. The traditional tones of the buildings of the valley echo intensely from these surfaces and from their joints and cut edges: the dark brown of the weathered wooden facades, the chalky white of their bright windows, and the oxblood red of the sparsely applied facade decoration. A broad sweeping stair climbs to the rehearsal area and descends to the plant room and other secondary spaces. Its striking dark balustrade of vertical rounded oak slats awakens memories of a xylophone. The somberly intense colors of the stair hall prepare us to enter the calm underlying atmosphere of the Klangräume, where the tone is set by the surfaces of beech plywood. Beech is a native timber that is rarely employed in building due to its capacity to shrink and is often only used as firewood. But it is also especially suitable in the form of the plywood that is required here for acoustic reasons. The white cut edges of the openings in the walls of the central space, which recall the sound holes of the hammered dulcimer, stand out particularly effectively against its steamed, reddish shimmering surface.

This "central space" is the most important one for music; all the other areas are grouped around it. But as the largest space it is also the most intimate and introverted; only the three window elements that provide access to the external stages offer limited glimpses into the surrounding landscape. The space is illuminated naturally via three skylights that hang obliquely in the roof around the central element. Elliptical below and circular above, these irradiate the space like overdimensioned spotlights. When we gaze up into the openings, the conic objects appear to be dancing in the space.

The reference to the concert hall in Isfahan, whose volumetric walls enhance the spatial acoustics by being constructed as hollow bodies with sound holes, plays a central role in Marcel Meili's propositions →. During the design process, the volumetric walls of the Klanghaus, which are heavily based on this Persian model, took on a stronger local character when the floral ornament that is stamped into the resonator of the hammered dulcimer, an instrument that is widespread in the region, was incorporated as the motif for the sound holes. Only later did it become clear that this motif had originally arrived in the valley on instruments from Persia, a discovery that exemplifies the productive cultural transfer embodied by the Klanghaus →. So-called acoustic mirrors are hidden in the structural cavities behind the perforated surfaces, their diverse metal surfaces shimmering through the openings →. The extraordinary acoustic quality of the space owes much not only to the various sound-absorbing panels from which these structural cavities are made, but also to their dimension, composition, and orientation. As we move through the space it becomes a walkable, interactive playable instrument. The floor is finished with oak end grain blocks due to the infinitesimal acoustic contribution of the vertical air columns trapped in the end grain. In addition to this, three resonance fields incorporated into the raised floor help to shape the sound within the space by reacting to the movement of feet or altering the sound of instruments as they are placed on the ground. These details enable the space and the sound to be "discovered like an objet trouvé" →.

→ Contribution by Axel Langer, p. 36

→ Contribution by Astrid Staufer, p. 122

→ Contribution by Matthias Ruf, p. 54

→ Marcel Meili, *Thesis Competition*, p. 24

The character of the ceiling is defined by a regular timber framework infilled with wooden panels that are inclined at different angles. The rigorous avoidance of parallel surfaces prevents flutter echoes and creates a variable acoustic image by ensuring that we hear sound waves coming from every possible direction. In the original project, this arched timber framework was conceived as a continuous, multi-directional substructure clad with coffered ceiling panels. Increasing cost pressure driven by rising timber prices (the estimate dated back to 2013) led to lengthy discussions during the cooperative tender process, and eventually to the decision to separate the structure and the finish of the ceiling and to replace this substructure with a two-directional system of linear supports, a decision that led to considerable savings.

Fig. 9

Fig. 10

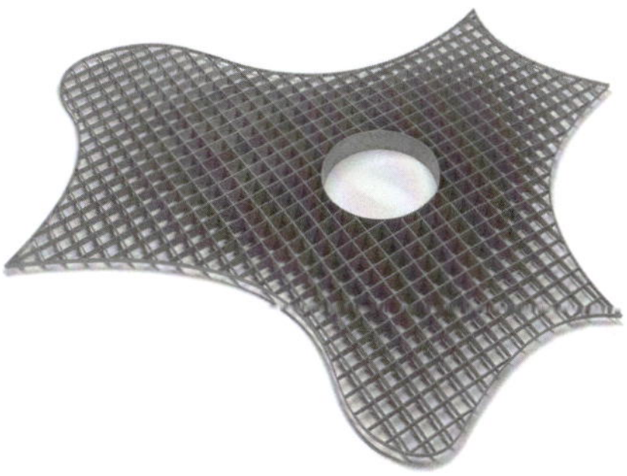

Fig. 11

Fig. 12

Fig. 13

Fig. 14

Fig. 9
View of the ceiling in the Schwendisee music room, featuring openable ceiling flaps that allow natural cross ventilation between the post-and-rail facade and the rooftop crown.

Fig. 10
Adjustment of the three resonance fields in the floor of the central space. Their raised floor construction resembles that of a stage—as light as possible, made up of large elements supported by a limited number of rubber bearings.

Fig. 11
Model photo of the multi-directional, lens-shaped roof truss, designed to cover the layout (execution project).

Fig. 12
Aerial view of the completed roof surface of EPDM sheeting, with fixing clamps and pan lids. The metal-clad rooftop crown houses the outlets for both natural ventilation and rear ventilation of the roof construction, while also framing the four skylights.

Fig. 13
View from the central space towards the roof structure during the erection process. The conical stumps of the four prefabricated, insulated skylights are already in place.

Fig. 14
View into the substructure of the skylights within the central space, before the application of the twisted three-ply paneling lining. Some of the ceiling joists have already been assembled.

Fig. 15

Fig. 16

Fig. 17

Fig. 18

Fig. 19

Fig. 20

Fig. 15
View inside the low-ceilinged parlor, with seating arranged for course participants to enjoy their refreshments. The ceiling is framed by panels covered in baker's linen, complemented by arrangements of hanging ceiling lights.

Fig. 16
The loggia features open arrays of folding shutters beneath slightly protruding panels that act as guardrails to the Iltios music room, recalling the small canopies typically found on the facades of the traditional local buildings.

Fig. 17
View through a box window from the control room into the central space, with the "Isfahan doors" open.

Fig. 18
View from the central space into the echo room through the open door. The prow of the room is highlighted by a small skylight, which can also be used for cascade ventilation.

Fig. 19
The building's entirely white underworld, with stalactite-like arrangements of electrical components within ceiling recesses and artisanal ornamentation in the sand-lime brickwork.

Fig. 20
View from the Schafberg music room towards the Schafberg, one of the peaks of the Alpstein massif. The convex curved post-and-rail facade embraces the landscape, allowing it to become present within the space.

These wooden supports, which are detailed to have optimal spans, are also better able to accommodate the large ducts that are part of the system of natural ventilation and rise towards the crown of the roof. The decision to ventilate all the musical spaces naturally was taken together with the users. No mechanical noise should compromise the acoustic experience. Fresh air flows into the building through motorized air vents next to the windows, which are protected by mesh for night cooling and can be operated individually during the day. The warm air that rises in the spaces is drawn towards the crown of the roof—directly in the central space and indirectly via ducts with dampers from the other spaces—and released to the outside. This decision to accept higher humidity levels in summer or unusually low temperatures in winter while the spaces are being ventilated was taken, together with the users, in order to avoid cutting the building off from the natural environment out of which it emerged and of which it wishes to remain a part.

Relationship with the landscape

Three further volumes cluster around the central space, pointing like fingers towards the landscape to which they open up via large areas of glazing. Realized as polygonal curves that are formed as a series of window elements in order to optimize the acoustics, these glazed facades appear to embrace the landscape. Due to their size they are the only significant metal elements in the building. Tectonically articulated and colorfully painted, they are divided horizontally, with a lower part that consists of smaller openable elements with folding shutters, and acts as a filter to the landscape in order to maintain the intimate character of the space and focus attention on the acoustic interaction. Above this, large glazed elements open up the view of the mountain peaks. The wall paneling in these spaces is more reserved; horizontal, vertical, and partly manipulated wooden slats structure the surfaces, which are filled with timber and textile elements with a range of acoustic qualities. The fact that these surfaces can be easily dismantled means that it will be possible to “tune” the spaces in future.

The resonance wall between the central space and the Schwendisee music room can be opened completely by theatrically pushing aside the so-called “Isfahan doors.” The resulting expansion of the spatial volume radically changes not only our acoustic perception of the central space but also the character of the space itself due to its new relationship with the landscape. This landscape becomes the stage of a previously introverted auditorium. But the acoustic impact of the central space can also be altered by opening the door to the “Echoraum,” which has yet another completely different acoustic and, thanks to a small skylight, a mystical and almost sacred atmosphere.

The volume facing the end of the valley is divided into two levels. The lower level contains a cozy and convivial "parlor" of a type that is familiar to local musicians. Above this, a rehearsal room faces the setting sun across a loggia, while two box-like windows on the opposite wall open up the view through the central space towards the Schwendisee. The rehearsal room, like most of the spaces in the Klanghaus, is thus open to multiple references. The parlor can be used for making music and as a visitor space that can also host a large buffet prepared in the adjacent kitchen. All the other support spaces, such as the artists' dressing rooms and the bathrooms are located in the economically designed, whitewashed basement, which is enlivened by some playful marble inlay and by "stalactites" that hang from the ceiling and contain technical items such as the smoke detectors.

Externally, the three wings form concave parabolas, whose vertices accommodate the accesses from the central space onto the forecourt and the two external stages. In a process modelled on the air-defense structures illustrated in the propositions, these stages gather, amplify, and focus the sounds coming from the landscape, creating astonishing acoustic effects. Fascinatingly, the three wings produce very different acoustic spaces: birdsong and animal noises intensify in the recess facing Schwendisee, while the sound of rushing water is more apparent on the side facing the stream. This means that music can be made in an intense dialogue with nature on both stages. And both are accessible from the central space via French doors; conversely, when these doors are open, the various sounds and strains of nature can be drawn into the central space ➔.

➔ Contribution by Lea Hagmann, Sonja Lieberherr-Schnyder, p. 94

The external facade is completely covered with manually split spruce shingles, while the three-dimensionally curved roof soffits are finished with small round shingles that were split by machine ➔. The way in which this screen wall of shingles was laid almost appears to allow the vibrant inner life and musicality of the Klanghaus to "push through" to the outside. An acoustic ornament was incorporated into the process of laying the shingles by hand in the form of small deviations in the position of the shingles that generate a subtle, optical shimmer. The walls end beneath an overhanging roof, whose edge is finely chiseled in the artisanal tradition, giving the building the air of a precious instrument. Several visual-aural surprises that allow visitors to enjoy "discovering the objet trouvé" despite the consistent cost pressure include the "incorrect use" of dark fiber cement roof tiles as a robust curved cladding to the base of the building and the cheap pan lids from a large Swiss manufacturer that act as visually vibrant snow guards on the black bitumen rubber roof. These trigger associations with traditional silver jewelry and also welcome visitors at the entrance door.

➔ Contribution by Susanna Koeberle, p. 102

Abstract-concrete idea

According to Adolf Loos, every building begins with an "idea": "He built them an idea there," wrote Karl Kraus, referring to the building designed by his friend on Michaelerplatz in Vienna.[3] This initial abstract concept is often simplified in the architecture and then called an "idea"—but this misinterprets Loos's proposition of the concrete idea; the task of the design and construction process is to constantly make this idea more "concrete." There is an automatic assumption that an idea is something of great purity and that whenever it is realized, whether successfully or otherwise, it is always weakened and can never achieve the power of the abstract idea. Marcel Meili's conceptual thinking and the architecture that this produces demonstrate that this assumption is far too simple. His idea is both abstract and concrete, just like the resulting built architecture. The abstract idea of a connection between architecture and landscape becomes the concrete shaping of a view from the space. In the concrete reference to the concert hall in Isfahan the forms are able to become traditional hammered dulcimers—and, from there, to transition further into abstract ornaments and patterns. In this sense they are an interpretation of cultural transfer. This abstract-concrete idea creates a foundation for broadly based communication at every level of architecture and for negotiating democratically in dialogue with all participants. "The final architecture could also look completely different."[4] Architecture is not conceived on the basis of a form but, rather, materializes during the process of its realization. This architecture is not self-important but it is understood to be important. For me, this is Marcel Meili's legacy.

This text is based on a group dialogue involving Astrid Staufer and Matthias Ruf (architecture), Hermann Blumer and Christoph Meier (structural engineering), Andreas Mühlebach (building physics and acoustics), Richard Widmer (natural ventilation), Sacha Vaucher (client project leader), Simone Hess (construction management), and Stephan Bischof (timber building) as well as on several one-on-one conversations with Astrid Staufer.

3 Karl Kraus. "Das Haus auf dem Michaelerplatz," in "Glossen," in *Die Fackel*, 313/314, Vienna 1910, p. 5, transl. by R.H. https://fackel.oeaw.ac.at/index.html?lang=de (accessed on February 23, 2025).

4 Meili 2010, proposition 6, p. 30, here p. 23.

A Walkable Instrument. On the Ideas Swirling Around in the Heads of the Architects of Sound

Matthias Ruf

Can a building be an instrument? And would spending time in an instrument be an acoustically engaging experience? Being inside a violin would certainly be unbearable for our ears. Unlike an enclosed built space—architecture—an instrument should be made to vibrate, to resonate. With architecture, the principle is exactly the opposite, because the essential requirements for a building that offers optimal spatial acoustics are solid, heavy walls and slabs. An instrument, on the other hand, is shaped from thin pieces of wood. For example, the ceiling of a violin is made of spruce, as knot-free as possible, straight, and not grown too quickly, marked by tightly packed annual rings. Such wood is very light, since the dark annual rings from the nutrient-poor winter are barely visible. It is light, highly elastic, has no internal tension, and is felled at the right time, during a waning moon.

The Klanghaus is also built of wood, the most accessible material in Toggenburg. The only materials found in the interior—besides the solid spruce and beech of the linear components—are semi-finished products such as the plywood and three-ply boards for the flat elements. Fiberboard was avoided due to its lack of elastic force and vibration capacity. This is why bass absorbers consist of thin and light panels, in contrast with point absorbers, where the grid, the size of the opening, the rear cavity, and any insulation play a role. Here, however, the soundwaves first make contact with the space via the floor finish. The oak end-grain flooring, with its microscopic vertical air columns, enriches the acoustic qualities. Compared to instrument-making however, the growth properties of the wood are far less significant.

In contrast, it is the forms or, so to speak, the body of the building that are more important for its design. According to Andres Bosshard, the three oversized corner columns that project into the central space are adapted from the spatial disposition of three large tree trunks, whose

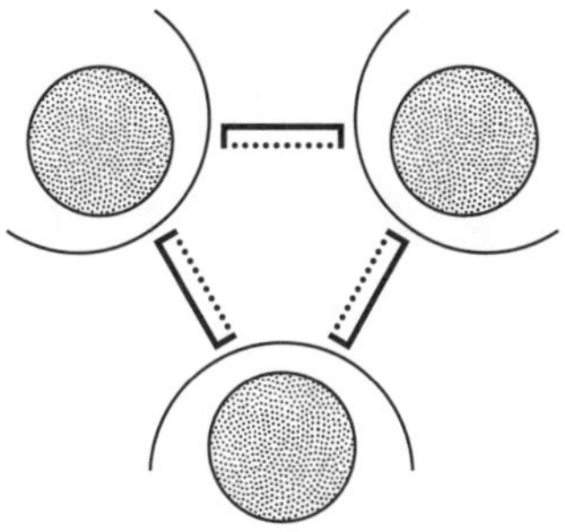

Fig. 1

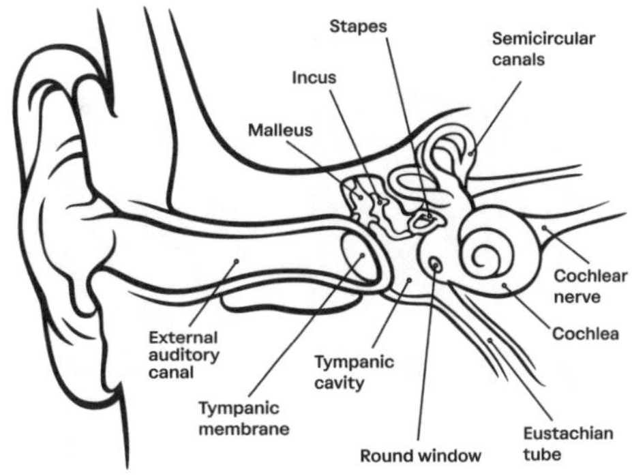

Fig. 2

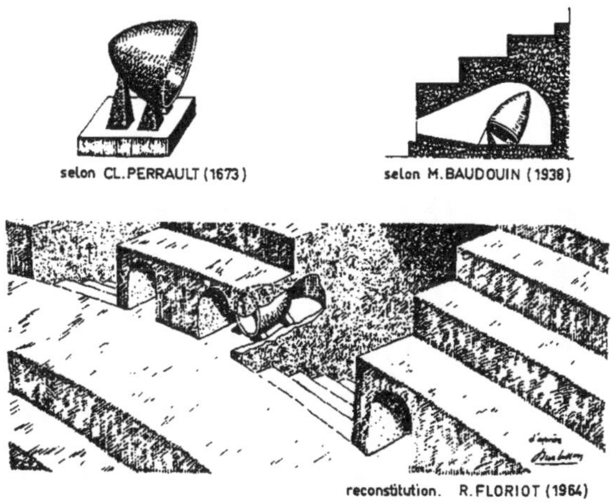

Fig. 3

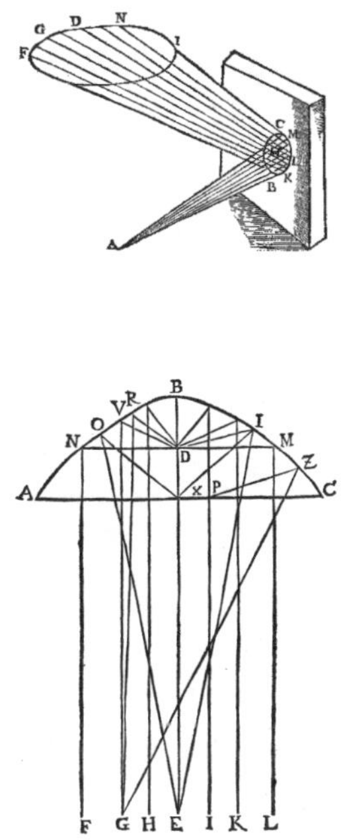

Fig. 4

Fig. 5

Fig. 1
Diagram showing the principle of three tree trunks, which shape the central space, and, between them, the perforated, spatial "Isfahan walls."

Fig. 2
Structure of the human ear with the oval and round windows.

Fig. 3
Three images reconstructing an "echea," the antique predecessor to the acoustic vase as described by Vitruvius.

Fig. 4
In *Phonurgia Nova*, which was published in 1673, Athanasius Kircher was the first to attempt to draw an analogy between the spreading of light waves and the propagation of sound. His bold ideas anticipated many of the laws applied by modern acoustics to the propagation of sound and opened the way for the vision of the "Ars Phonocamptica," which recognized the causal relationship between sound and space and conceptualized the essence of spatial sound as "Phonurgia Nova" (literally: the new art of the sound smith). (Andres Bosshard, 2025).

Fig. 5
Central space in the Klanghaus, canopy with the four "celestial ears" and the inscribed letter A.

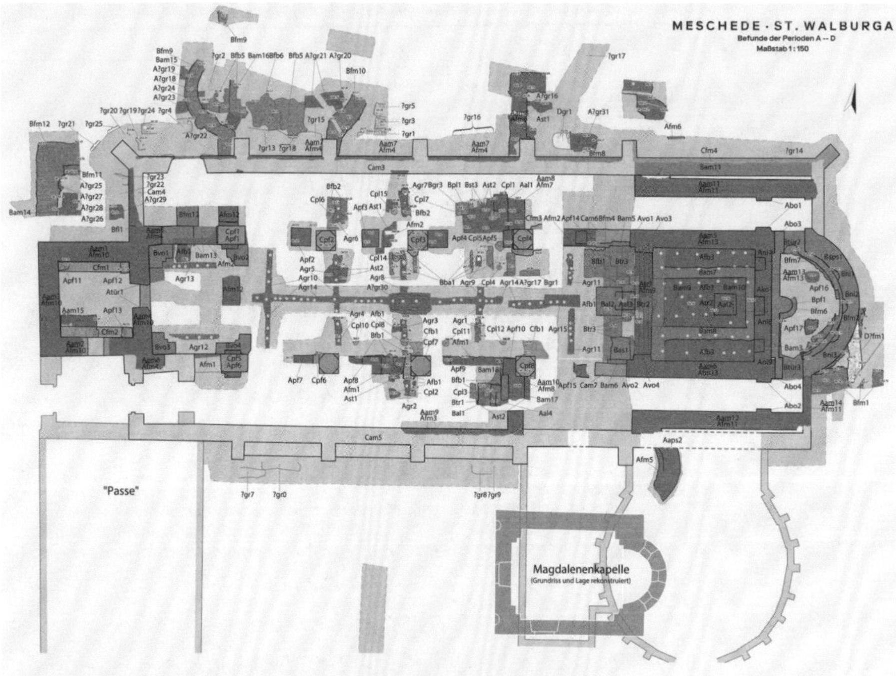

Fig. 6

Fig. 7

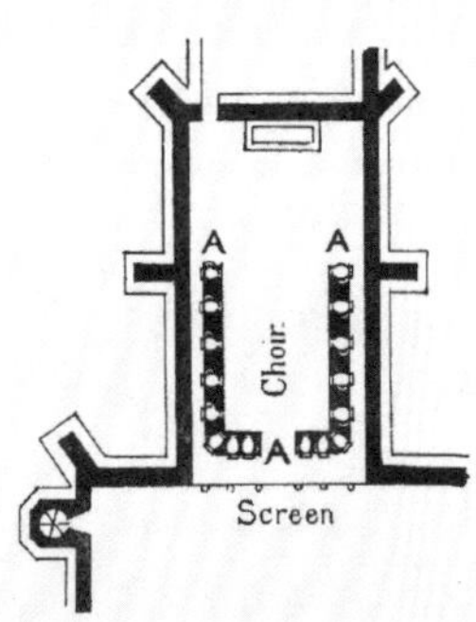

Fig. 8

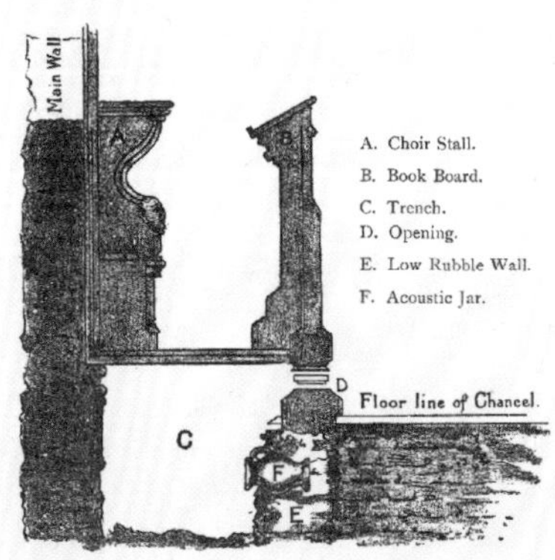

Fig. 9

Fig. 10a

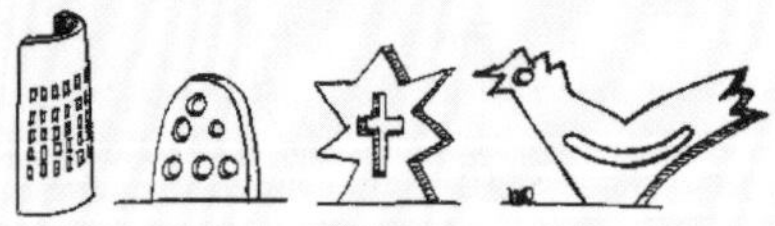

Fig. 10b

Fig. 6
Plan of the excavations at St. Walburga in Meschede; the yellow circles denote the acoustic vessels discovered in, among other areas, the nave and side aisles and in the choir.

Fig. 7
Choir with later ceiling in the convent church of Oetenbach in Zurich, acoustic vessels from the early sixteenth century and painting from the fifteenth and sixteenth centuries (photograph dated 1903).

Fig. 8
Two L-shaped groups of acoustic vessels buried in trenches below the choir stalls of St. Peter Parmentergate in Norwich.

Fig. 9
Section through the choir stalls of St. Peter Parmentergate in Norwich.

Figs. 10a and 10b
Various forms of wolf's tile found on roofs in the Massif Central. A warning wind instrument that generates a sound when activated by the continental cold air from Siberia that can drive wolves into the village.

crowns compose the roof. Their convex forms enable them to optimally distribute the sound within the space. Between them are the perforated, spatial "Isfahan walls." They prevent the uniform reflection of the sound, maximize resonance times, and create a high degree of diffusion. The upper areas of wall are further modulated by a variety of elements that enable the sound to rise.

The gently convex ceiling, formed by coffers with inclined infills, rises from its center towards the three wings and the mountainous landscape beyond. The sound is scattered by the intermediate panels. Parallel surfaces that would generate flutter echoes, or cross-sections resembling the spaces below gable roofs that could create unwelcome focal points, were avoided as much as possible. The canopy at the heart of the space, which combines four upward-facing skylights, resembling "celestial ears," directs the sound towards the three external walls that penetrate the central space. The clashing soundwaves merge, intensify, weaken, or overlap and, hence, disperse completely.

Is it a serendipitous coincidence that the form of these skylights corresponds to the human anatomy? The fact is that the three obliquely angled skylights have the same form as the *fenestra vestibuli* (oval window) that transfers sound waves in our ears thanks to its membrane effect. And the *fenestra rotunda* (round window), which serves to decompress in the ear, ventilates the Klanghaus naturally by allowing air to escape. The Rotunda also references the architectural history of central space buildings, like those by Andrea Palladio. The letter "A" inscribed into the rotunda could allude to the Persian word *ava*, which means "sound." Or is it the "A" of German polymath Athanasius Kircher?

Rather than merely consisting of passive spatial components that are reflected in the forms and the structure, instruments also have active ones. Anyone who has read Vitruvius's *Ten Books of Architecture* will recall the passage in the fifth chapter of the fifth book about bronze acoustic vases—*echea*. These should have been placed below the rows of seats in the theater to create a natural echo that would compensate for the lack of a roof—although none has ever been found. What was uncovered, however, were ceramic vessels from sites such as the ancient theater in Nora, as well as early medieval churches including St. Walburga in Meschede (at least 139 vessels) or Oetenbach Nunnery in Zurich (at least 68). Given that they were made from burnt clay, these traditional jars probably functioned more as acoustic resonators than as receptacles, a conclusion that is also suggested by the fact that they were built into vaults and the walls of choirs. By reversing sound amplitudes, in a similar way to noise-cancelling headphones, these so-called Helmholtz resonators are able to eliminate certain frequencies; however, by connecting spaces, they can also reinforce

Fig. 11

Fig. 12

Fig. 13

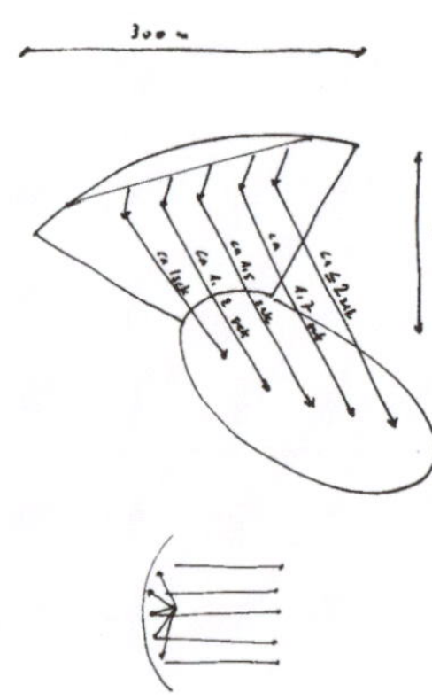
Fig. 14

Fig. 15

Fig. 16

Fig. 11
The first experiments with suspended sheets of bronze in David Fuchs's metal workshop in Deggenhausen; Andres Bosshard with the measuring device, August 2013.

Fig. 12
Limpe and Paul Fuchs experimenting with a sheet of bronze in Harry Bertoia's workshop together with their daughter, while David takes the photograph. Between their heads, the rectangular hollow gong that acts as a model for the reverb cushion; to the right, Bertoia's chimes, 1981.

Fig. 13
Andres Bosshard, *Riflessione di una Diga*, dam wall concert in Fusio, Valle Maggia. The visualization shows the loudspeakers hanging from the edge of the dam wall and their downward reflections.

Fig. 14
Conceptual sketch describing the generation of a monumental acoustic reflection that projects the music to the audience and the musicians at the foot of the dam wall with a second's delay. Depending upon the concentration and orientation, the sound can be perceived at distances of up to 10 km.

Fig. 15
Andres Bosshard, *Klanghimmel MQ* above the MuseumsQuartier in Vienna, 2011 (part of the *TONSPUR_expanded. Der Lautsprecher* exhibition in freiraum quartier21 INTERNATIONAL). Satellite dishes tower above the cornice of the entrance building.

Fig. 16
The loudspeakers installed at the focal points of the satellite dishes project the sound into the courtyard of the complex.

sound—as exemplified by the act of blowing into the mouth of a bottle. And yet, we can only speculate about the contribution made by the pots that are geometrically arranged below the floor of the nave and aisles and underneath the choir stalls. They suggest the acoustic intensification of theatrical moments during processions, or of seated choirs. According to Bosshard, early medieval builders were also aware of the auratic effect of bottles that were built into the ridge of a roof, generating ghostly tones as the wind whistled by. Further examples of traditional wind instruments include the wolf's tile illustrated here.

The wealth of experience described above triggered the first experiments by David Fuchs—Bosshard's inventive helpmate since their first collaboration for Expo 2000 in Bad Pyrmont and Hannoversch Münden—in his metal workshop in Deggenhausen. Having initially experimented with bent metal and suspended panels, his next phase of development was decisively influenced by experiences from journeys across America taken in his youth with his artist parents. A visit to see Harry Bertoia building acoustic sculptures in the 1980s encouraged Fuchs, over thirty years later, to experiment with hollow metal objects. Bosshard had already been infected with "parabola influenza" during his project on the dam wall in Fusio, Valle Maggia, in 1987.

A second stage of development then saw the birth of two innovations: the reverb cushion and the acoustic mirror. The echo cushions consisted of two rectangular sheets of steel with a thickness of 0.5 millimeters that were inflated using compressed air—and later hydraulic pressure—and suspended in a mobile frame. The acoustic mirrors were built by welding together folded segments of two-millimeter-thick bronze sheet to form dishes that we can see glinting deep within the cavities of the "Isfahan walls." The steel cushions can generate a voluminous echo with a neutral tone, while the bronze mirrors, in addition to having a rich overtone spectrum, have shape-defined focal points that can be aligned in the room. They act as transmitters and their spatial presence can be enhanced by increasing the degree of opening of the "Isfahan doors." The materiality of the mirrors lends the central space its specific resonance profile, subtly coloring it in a similar way to yellow paper placed in front of the cold bulb of an office lamp.

A form of mountain echo with a delay ranging between one and twelve seconds, a length of time that almost exactly matches that of the existing Alpine panorama, can be heard resonating in the central space. Despite the spatial boundaries, the fading sound creates an atmosphere that appears diametrically opposed to that of an enclosed volume: the spatial limits are broken. The acoustic mirrors honor the idea and the principal requirement of making music that, like the Alpine blessing, is oriented towards the mountains and the landscape, whilst covered overhead. Before the referendum, the advisory committee of the Cantonal Council had implemented savings that would have impacted upon the artistic content of the project. But this project involves acoustic art that is integral to the Klanghaus experiment. If the first official act following the relaunch of the project had not been to correct this error, the Klanghaus would have almost lost its soul. According to tradition, frugal clients, such as those whose topping-out ceremonies are too sober, are still punished to this day by having empty bottles built into their gable walls—creating a soul-destroying howling that will pursue them for the rest of their lives. We have yet to discover anything of this sort, except for a larch shingle in the spruce cladding.

The essay was written on the basis of conversations with Andres Bosshard and David Fuchs that freely explored their research into acoustic ideas.

Fig. 17

Fig. 18

Fig. 19

Fig. 20

Fig. 21

Fig. 22

Fig. 17
Two sheets of steel are welded together and expanded using hydraulic pressure—at these greater dimensions this is far less dangerous than compressed air.

Fig. 18
The serial pressing of metal is too complex and expensive, as a result of which the acoustic mirrors are produced in segments. The connections are fully welded to ensure that they do not "rattle." The dimensions of the reverb cushions are initially relatively small before these are expanded using compressed air.

Fig. 19
Second development: a bronze mirror and reverberation cushions, and parabolic dish for long-distance communication in the background.

Fig. 20
Completed acoustic mirror. In the center, one can see that the edges of the bronze sheet do not touch. Folded rims give them extra stability.

Fig. 21
Spot welds on the rear hold the segments together. The intricate sequencing of this welding anticipates excess distortion.

Fig. 22
Hanging and adjustment of the acoustic mirrors in the space. The focal points of the mirrors are spatially arranged within the Klanghaus with the help of powerful spotlights.

Sectional perspectives 1

1 Roof surface of EPDM sheeting (synthetic rubber)
2 Non-penetrative fixing clamps
3 Pan lids as snow guards
4 Box gutter with metal drip edge
5 Rooftop crown with double standing seam consisting of:
6 Outlet for natural ventilation
7 Outlet for rear ventilation with ventilation grille
8 Conic skylight with double standing seam
9 Linear laminated spruce roof structure
10 Recesses for layered insulation
11 Natural ventilation ducting
12 Prefabricated elements of rooftop crown
13 External wall elements consisting of:
14 Posts and hinged rails
15 Outlet for mechanical ventilation combined with skylight
16 Manually split rectangular spruce shingles with acoustic ornamentation
17 Fiber cement base cladding
18 Frame structure to canopy
19 Mechanically split round spruce shingles to roof soffit
20 External stage with larch deck
21 Ventilation opening in reveal
22 Openable skylight for natural cross ventilation

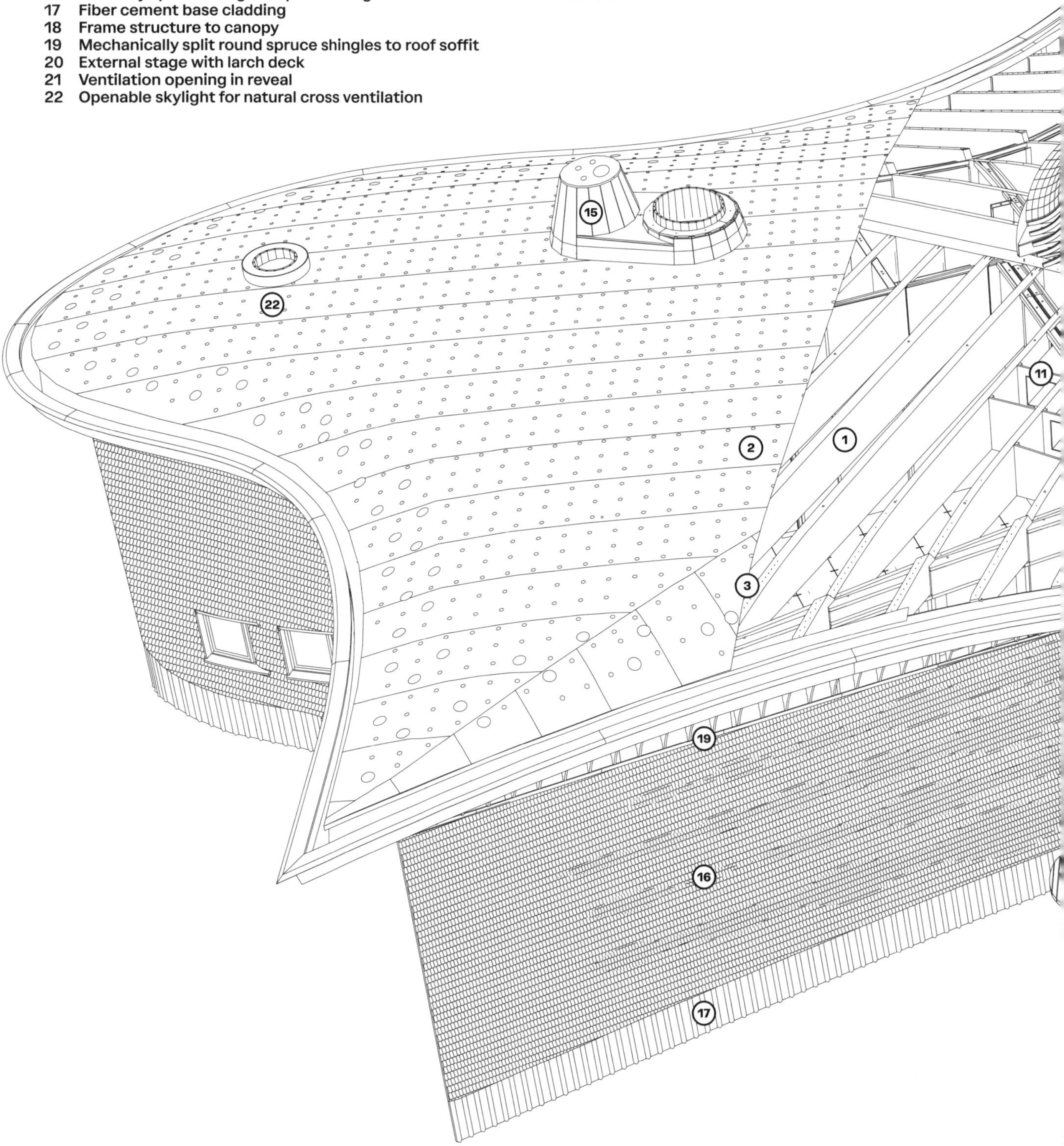

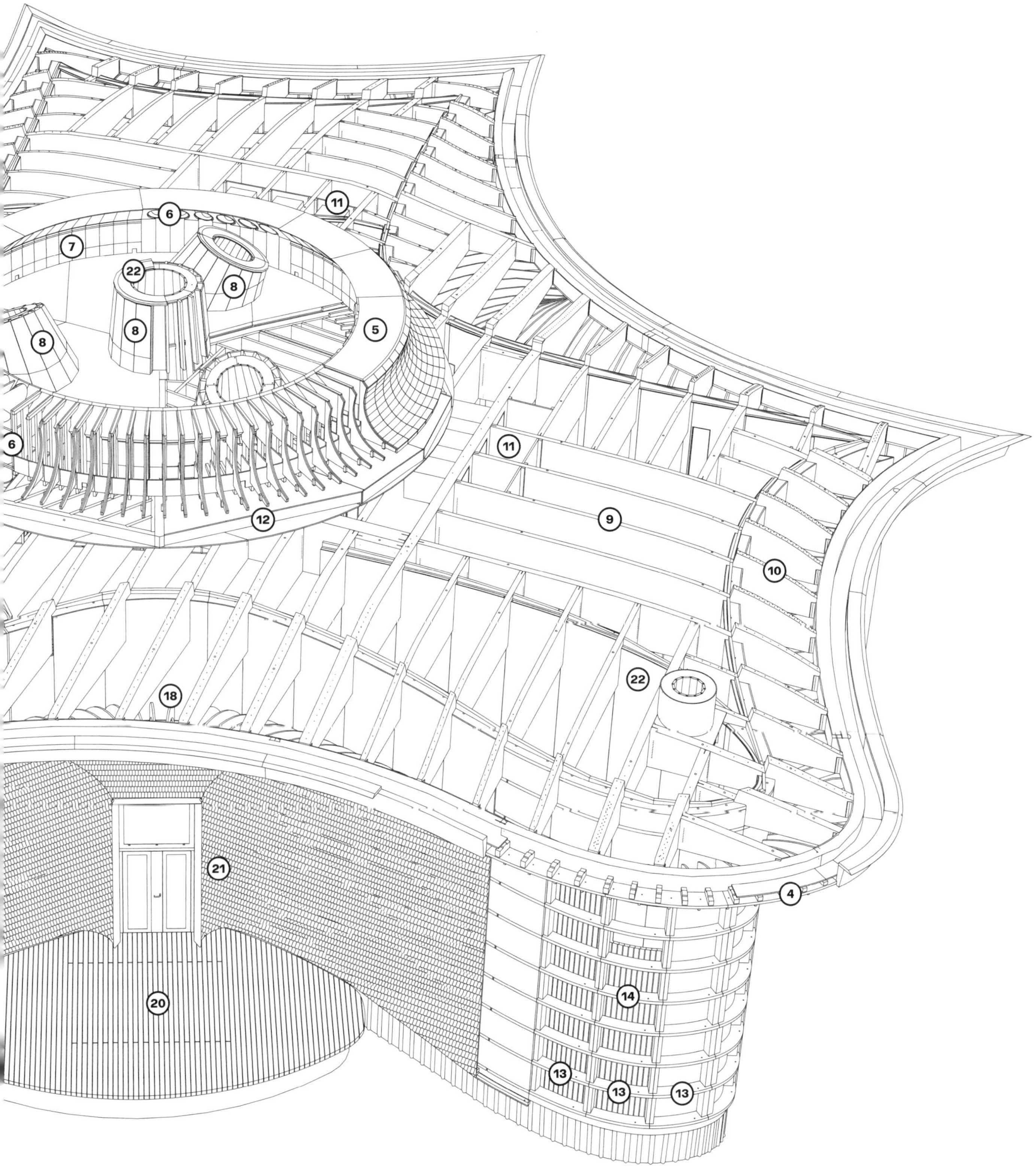
11
6
7
22
8
8
8
5
6
11
9
12
10
22
18
21
4
20
14
13
13
13

Sectional perspectives 2

1 Linear laminated spruce roof structure
2 Recesses for layered insulation
3 Natural ventilation ducting
4 Prefabricated elements of rooftop crown
5 Internal cladding to skylight
6 Frame structure to canopy
7 Mechanically split round spruce shingles to roof soffit
8 Ventilation opening in reveal
9 Openable skylight in central space
10 Ventilation opening in post-and-rail facade
11 Openable ceiling vents
12 Freely shaped coffered ceiling with inclined panels
13 “Isfahan walls” with acoustic mirrors
14 “Isfahan door” with acoustic mirrors
15 Beech plywood acoustic cladding to the music rooms
16 Schafberg staircase
17 Dressing rooms, WCs, storage areas, technical plant
18 Rainwater downpipe
19 Reduction of basement as money-saving measure

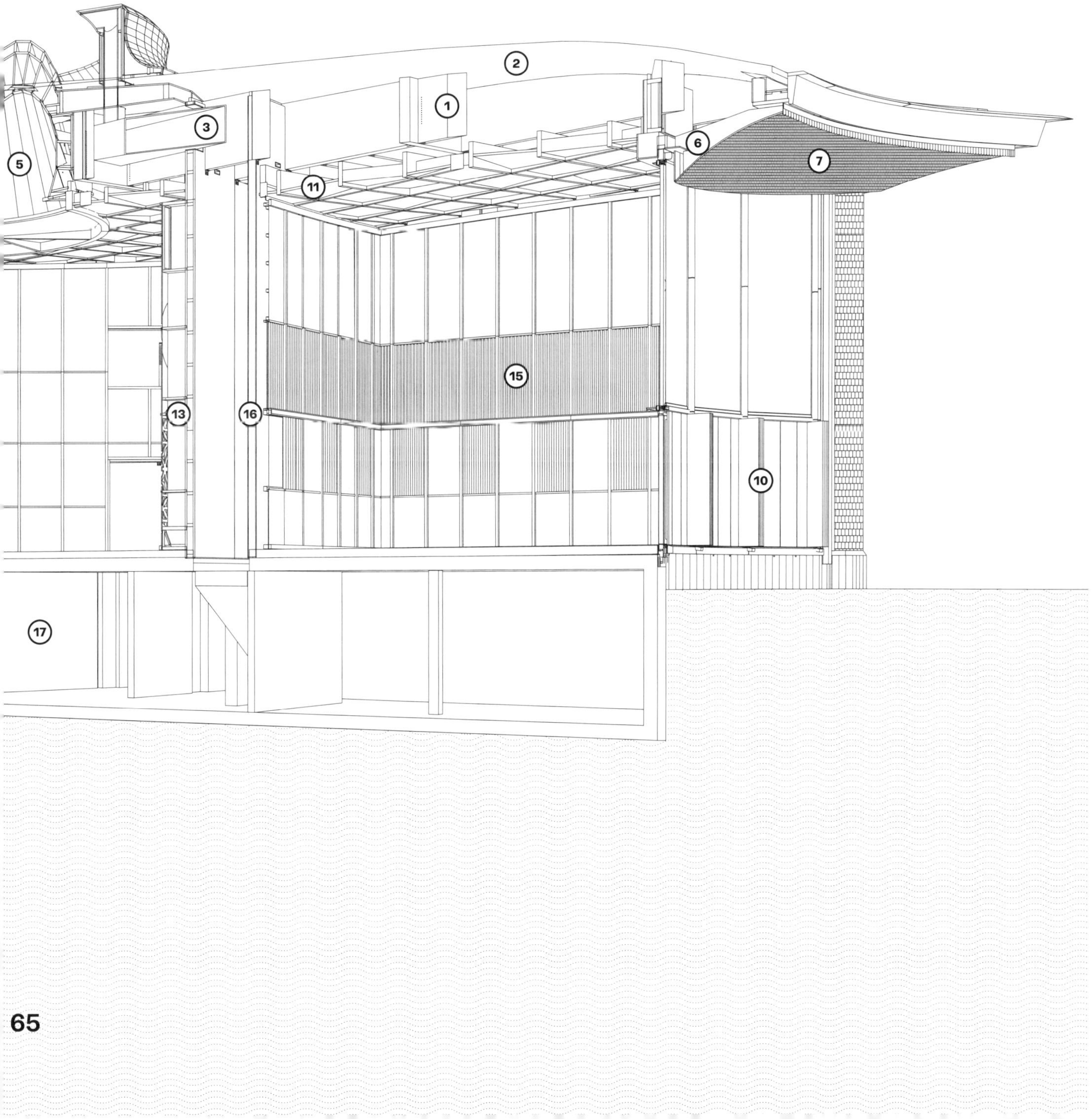
2
1
3
6
7
5
11
15
13
16
10
17

Ground floor

0 Forecourt
1 Entrance
2 Stair hall
3 Self-service buffet/kitchen/kiosk
4 Parlor
5 Loggia
6 Central space
7 Echo room
8 Schwendisee music room
9 Schafberg music room
10 External stages

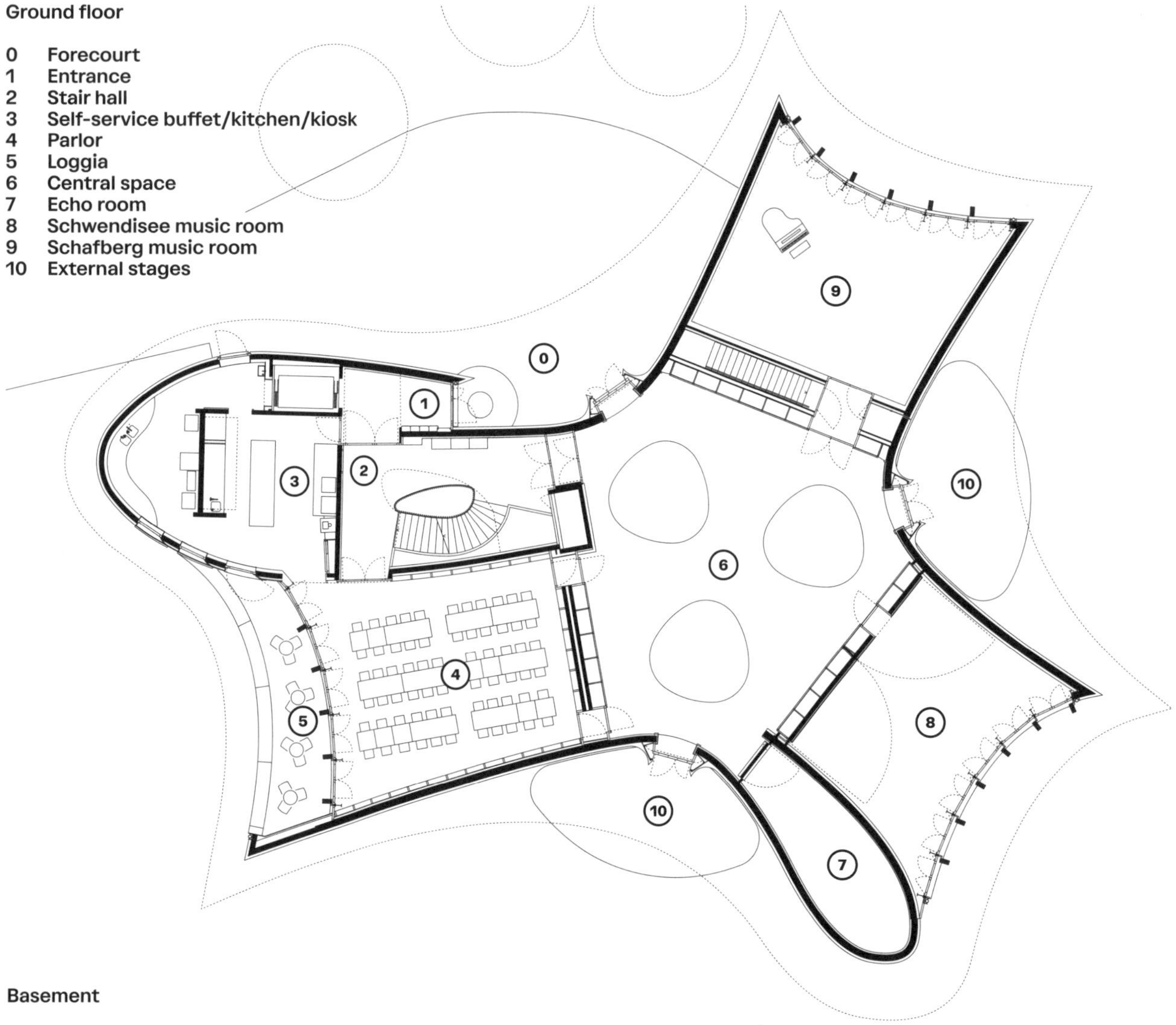

Basement

15 Dressing rooms
16 Materials store
17 Kitchen dishwashers/store
18 WCs
19 Janitor's room
20 Cleaners' room
21 Plant room

Upper floor

11 Iltios music room
12 Control room
13 Lütispitz room
14 Void above ground floor

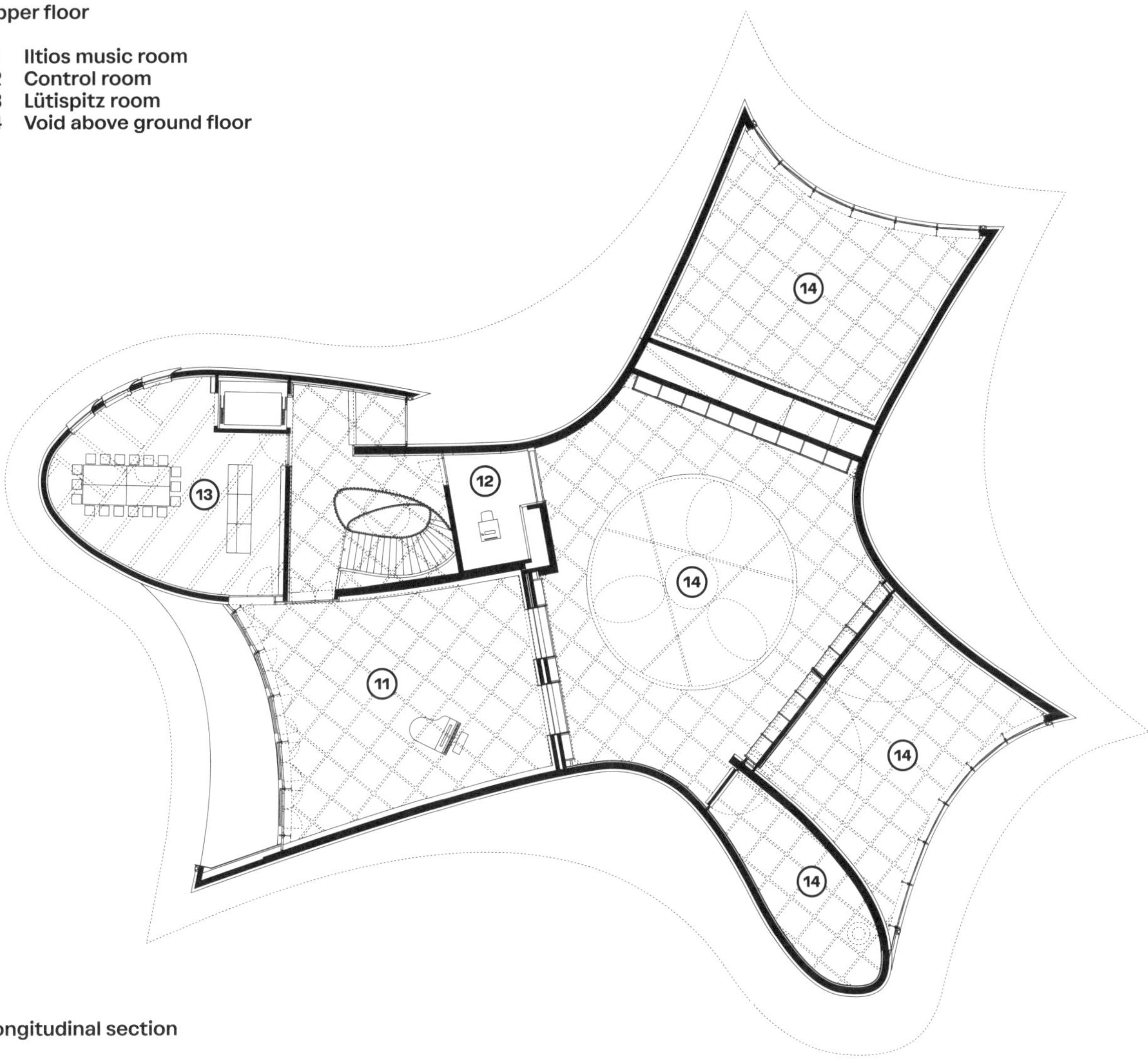

Longitudinal section

4 Parlor
5 Loggia
6 Central space
10 External stage
11 Iltios music room

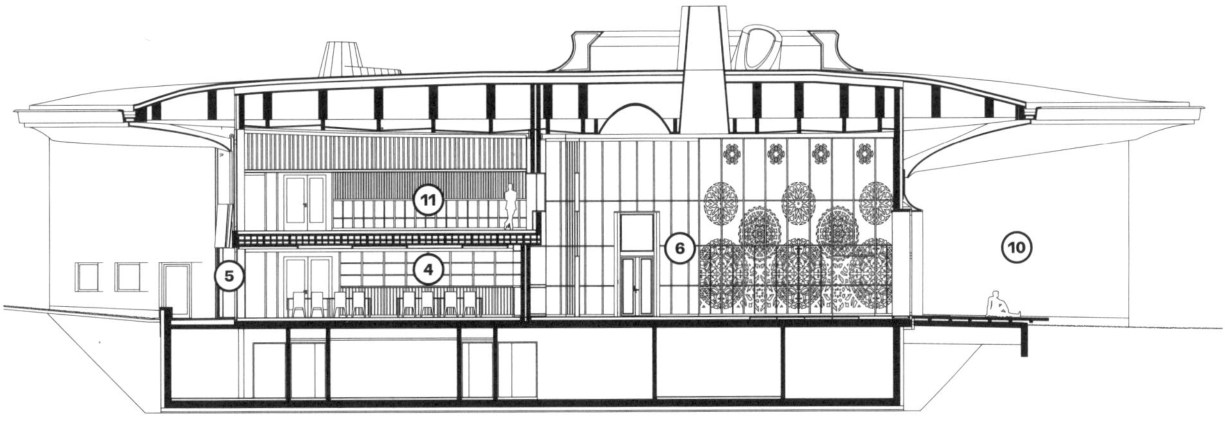

Ground floor execution plan

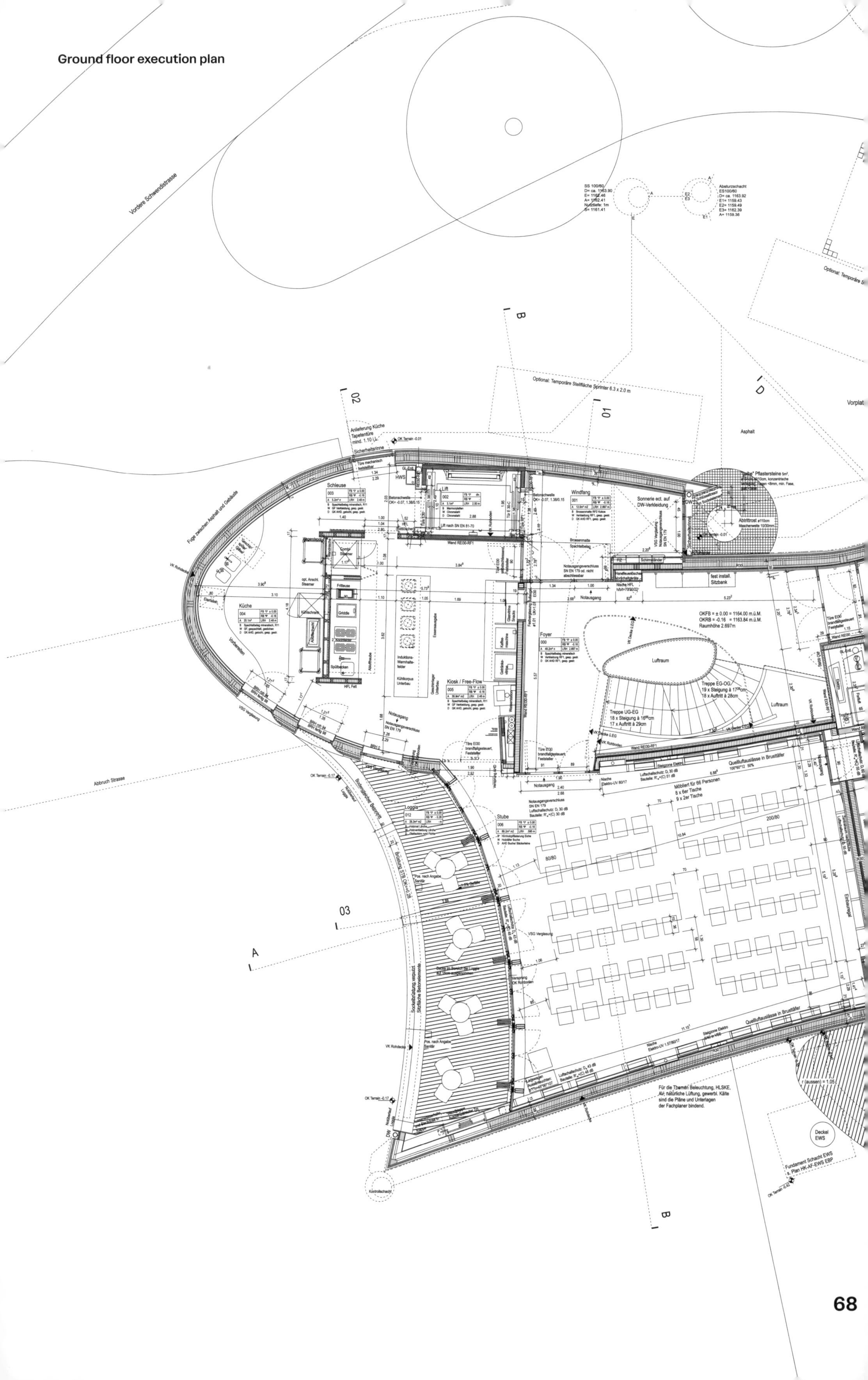

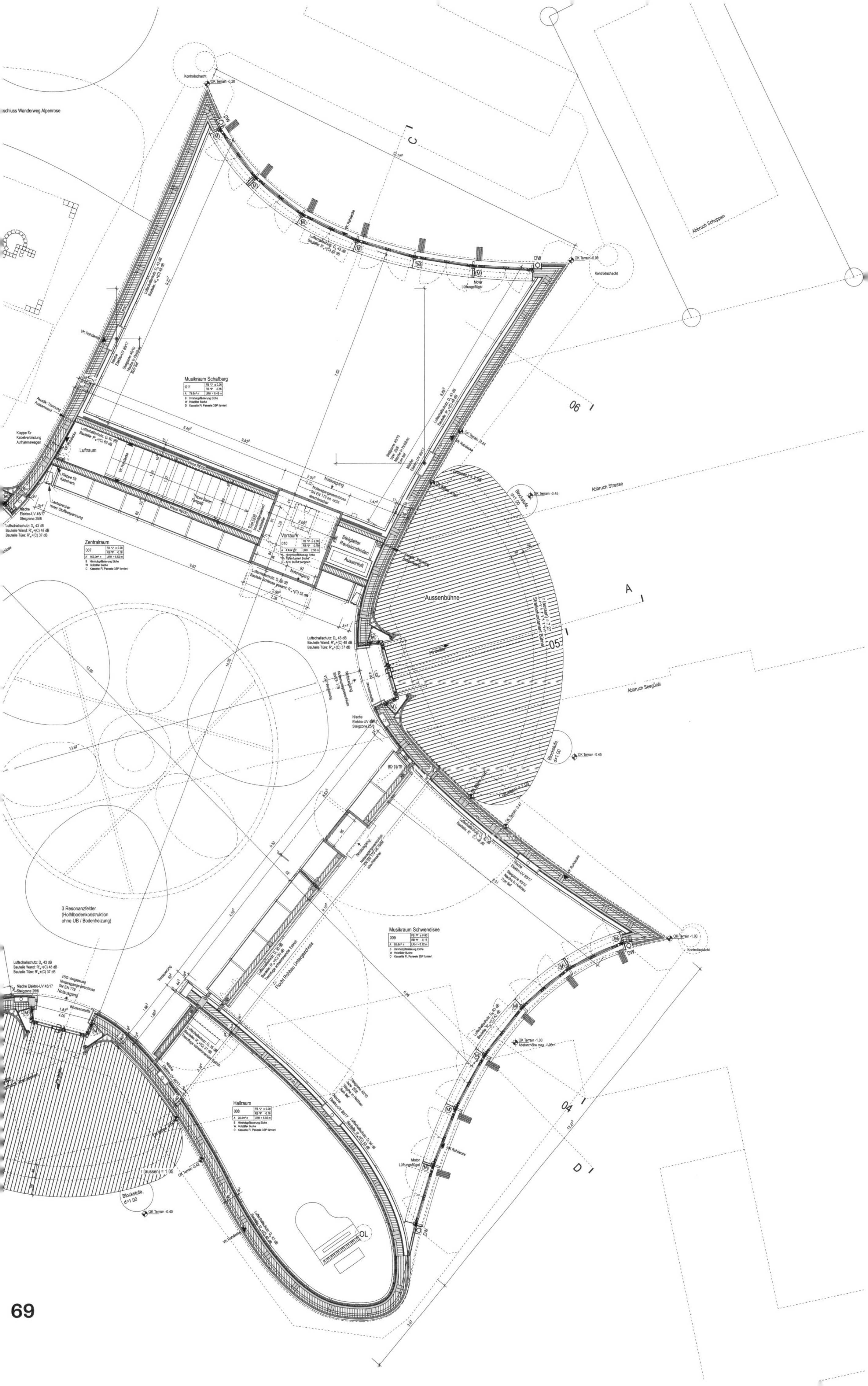

Musikraum Schafberg
Zentralraum
Luftraum
Vorraum
Steigleiter Revisionsboden
Aussenluft
Aussenbühne
Abbruch Strasse
Abbruch Seegüetli
Abbruch Schuppen
Kontrollschacht
Musikraum Schwendisee
Hallraum
3 Resonanzfelder (Hohlbodenkonstruktion ohne UB / Bodenheizung)
Blockstufe, d=1.00

The Klanghaus. An Essentially Social Project

Andrea Wiegelmann

The story of the Klanghaus is a story about a widely shared enthusiasm and about standing up for a project, regardless of the obstacles. It is a story of resonance, of music, of natural tones, and of sound.

Above the villages of Wildhaus and Unterwasser in Ober-toggenburg, at an altitude of 1,150 meters, there is a very special area of level moorland that contains the two Schwendisee lakes. The first lake, which faces the valley, offers a wonderful panoramic view of Säntis and the Wildhauser Schafberg. Not far from the shore of the lake, we now find the Klanghaus. Sitting in a hollow in the land-scape, the volume, with its convex and concave curves, is a resonator, a space for sound and for those dedicated to creating it.

Sound is an integral part of our perception

"Sound," says Peter Roth, musician, composer, and initiator of the Klanghaus, which is the latest component of his Klangwelt (Sound World), a concept that he developed together with engaged fellow enthusiasts, "is an integral part of our perception."[1] Here on the Schwendisee we can experience this at close hand. For Roth, this is a place where he can share what moves him. He speaks of his early experiences of sound, when he was out and about with his grandfather, of how the ringing of the cowbells and natural yodeling gave him goose bumps, of his relationship with sound and music and of his studies at the conser-vatoire in Zurich, which set him on the path towards the music of natural tones. Today's Klangwelt Foundation is built on five cornerstones: the Klangkurse (Sound Courses), which were offered from the very start, the Klangweg (Sound Trail), which opened in 2003, the Naturstimmen-festival (Festival of Natural Voices), which was established in 2004, the Klangschmiede (Sound Smith), which is home to the Klangwelt administration, and the youngest child, the Klanghaus (Sound House). These components, which

1 Conversation with Peter Roth on August 12, 2024.

Fig. 1

Fig. 1
Schwendisee with a view of the former Seegüetli seminar hotel.

are devoted to sound, natural tones, music, and the region, are part of a success story that, even if many obstacles had to be overcome, is committed, equally, to the culture and tradition of Obertoggenburg and to its exchanges with sound-based cultures worldwide. The Klanghaus provides a resonator for this musical and intercultural dialogue.

The Klanghaus is a very special project for Peter Roth, it embodies his feelings for space and sound

There would be no Klanghaus without Roth. "For me, the Klanghaus is very close to Peter Roth's heart, it embodies his sense of space and sound," explains Hans Schmid, who headed the Office for Culture of the Canton of St.Gallen from 2004 to 2007 and accompanied the fledgling project.[2] Schmid is convinced that personalities like Roth are essential if we are to realize such cultural projects. At the same time, the initiative was launched at the right moment. This was a period during which cultural policies in the canton began to pay more attention to the promotion of regional culture.

The Klanghaus can bring people together, sound has the potential to do this

Our story starts in 1973. Roth returns from his studies to Toggenburg, plays string music and free jazz with his own band, directs the choir of the Reformed Church in Alt St. Johann, and composes. He begins to offer courses on the traditional sounds and music of Toggenburg, overtone singing and shamanic cultures, and organizes singing weeks. He looks for a place where he can share these interests. Roth recalls his reasoning for the development of the Klanghaus project at this time: "Toggenburg has not been geared towards summer tourism for a long time. At the same time, it needs to offer something to the locals. The Klanghaus can bring people together, sound has the potential to do this."[3] His model is Monte Verità cultural

2 Conversation with Hans Schmid on July 30, 2024.

3 Conversation with Peter Roth on August 12, 2024.

center above Ascona. In 1993, the former Seegüetli nature lovers' center on the Vordere Schwendisee becomes the setting for his courses. But the building remains temporary and there is no room to make sounds.

At the turn of the millennium, Roth sets off on a trip around the world. Expo takes place in Hannover, for which the Graubünden architect Peter Zumthor builds the Swiss Pavilion, Klangkörper Schweiz. Planed larch and pine beams are piled up to form nine-meter-high walls that enclose courtyards, the Klangräume (Sound Spaces), which are occupied by accordion and dulcimer players with soloists and a variety of instruments. Roth visits Caplutta Sogn Benedetg in Sumvitg in Surselva, which was built by Zumthor in 1988. The wooden chapel has a tear-shaped floor plan and the basement, says Roth, is a resonator. The idea of creating a building for sound becomes more concrete. Roth speaks with Zumthor.

Something begins to move

In 2002, a cycle of concerts is launched to mark the 850th anniversary of the village of Alt St. Johann, Toggenburg, and the Alt St. Johann choir invites music groups from across Europe to perform. The concerts are a huge success and eventually lay the foundations for Roth's Naturstimmenfestival (Festival of Natural Voices), which first takes place in Alt St. Johann in 2004. Roth describes his motivation: "There is music based on natural tones in every culture; it is often herders who uphold these traditions and I wanted to encourage exchange between these cultures."[4] He composes *Ammann's Vermächtnis* (Ammann's Legacy), a musical play for children's choir, choir, and instruments. The work is inspired by the life of Toggenburg's Ulrich Ammann, a self-taught eighteenth-century instrument maker. In 2002, alongside the cycle of concerts and Roth's composition, one of Ammann's clarinets in the form of a walking stick is added to the collection of the Metropolitan Museum in New York. The positive mood creates fertile ground for the development of Roth's project. In the following year, the first section of the Klangweg is opened. Ebneter is able to show that the revenue of the mountain railway increases significantly during the summer season. The Klangwelt project is incorporated into the mission statement of the municipality of Alt St. Johann. According to Ebneter, it was fortunate that the municipal council also supported the project financially from the very start.

Culture is important for the identity in the canton

Peter Roth, who has also led the choir project in St.Gallen since 2022, wins the support of the then Cantonal Councilor Kathrin Hilber for his Klanghaus idea. It becomes a cantonal project. "It was a convergence of subjects that concerned me at the time," explains Hilber.[5] The Cantonal Councilor

4 Ibid.

5 Conversation with Kathrin Hilber on July 23, 2024.

recognizes the importance to the canton of supporting culture from both the economic and the social perspectives. She is committed to promoting the cultural strengths of rural regions. "The Klanghaus fitted in with this concept."[6] She finds an ally in Hans Schmid. Hilber and Schmid increase cultural funding in the Canton of St.Gallen. "Culture is important for the identity in the canton, it can attract people. We anchored this in the economic mission statement of the canton,"[7] explains Hilber, and Schmid adds: "This works differently in rural areas from the way it works in the city. Major projects must be jointly supported by the municipalities in the region. We established the platform Südkultur in order to encourage such cooperation. This enhanced the position of the Klanghaus."[8]

An opportunity to rethink the project

Zumthor designs an ensemble of buildings centered on a large hall made from spruce and maple. In 2007, the canton approves the preliminary project.[9] The Klangwelt Association had been established the year before, and in 2008, the Cantonal Government names the initiative as one of its five priorities for cultural funding.[10] A complaint by the architects' professional body against the direct commissioning of Peter Zumthor leads to the launch of an invited ideas competition. Zumthor withdraws from the process. Today, Roth speaks of this not as a setback but, rather, of an opportunity to rethink the building for the unique location on the Schwendisee. This approach says a lot about Roth and his passion for the project.

What is a Klanghaus?

The support of local politicians and the canton is decisive for the Klanghaus. The Cantonal Building Director Werner Binotto includes the Klanghaus in his budget. The public tender takes place in 2010. The selected form of tender—a competition between proposals—is a response to the vagueness of the program. Werner Binotto answers questions about the form of the tender: "How does one organize a competition for a building whose program is still open? The Klanghaus is not a concert hall; there is no spatial program for this special place. So we asked the participating offices how they would proceed; we looked for the best strategy."[11] Three questions were put to the ninety offices who responded to the tender: Who are you? What have you built? What is a Klanghaus? Then, six offices were selected to make propositions, including Meili, Peter Architekten from Zurich. At this office it is Meili who takes care of the project. "Marcel Meili came with a model to present his proposition," explains Roth, "a form consisting of concave and convex openings, a wooden instrument crouching in the hollow below the lake. It simply felt right."[12]
The jury chaired by Kathrin Hilber suggests that this entry should be developed further.

6 Ibid.

7 Ibid.

8 Conversation with Hans Schmid on July 30, 2024.

9 Amt für Kultur, Kanton St.Gallen (ed.), *Klanghaus. Ergebnisse des Vorprojekts*, 2008.

10 Alongside the Klangwelt, these are the Kunst(Zeug) Haus Rapperswil-Jona, the Genossenschaft Konzert und Theater St.Gallen, Schloss Werdenberg, and the Lokremise St.Gallen.

11 Conversation with Werner Binotto on July 25, 2024.

12 Conversation with Peter Roth on August 12, 2024.

Fig. 2

Fig. 2
Election poster for the Cantonal referendum, 2019. The Klanghaus Toggenburg is only approved at the second attempt. The first project is torpedoed in the final vote in the Cantonal Parliament in March 2016. Following this, an initiative committee is formed in the region with the aim of reclaiming the project for Toggenburg. In 2019, the electors of St.Gallen say *Ja* to the Klanghaus Toggenburg.

We are building a building for something that typically has no specific space

Katrin Meier, Hans Schmid's successor in the Office for Culture and also a member of the jury recalls: "It was Meili who had addressed the questions most profoundly. What is the music of natural tones, what is yodeling or an Alpine blessing, what is the musical tradition of Toggenburg? He developed an understanding for the type of building that can provide a space for these sounds."[13] She describes Meili's proposal: "We are building a building for something that typically has no specific space. The Klanghaus is something new. It is creating an experimental space for the music of natural tones. It is just as dedicated to tradition and custom as it is to development and experimentation."[14]

Meili adds a personal closing statement to his propositions: "I traveled quite a lot while carrying out this investigation. It became a journey to the heart of Swiss traditional music that wasn't planned as such."[15] And, to conclude, "This insight into a proud culture has taught me two things, including: only an architecture that is sure of its own rules is in a position to say anything at all to music."[16]

In this sense, his project is an architecture of sound. Meili develops the execution design with Staufer & Hasler Architekten from Frauenfeld. The task is now to generate enthusiasm among the people of Obertoggenburg for the youngest child of the Klangwelt. The foundation has already been laid by its economic success and the income from tourism earned by the region, but the Klanghaus reaches a different dimension by being a manifestly public place in the Klangwelt. And not everyone is happy about the attention that such a building can attract beyond the borders of the canton.

13 Conversation with Katrin Meier on July 29, 2024.

14 Ibid.

15 Marcel Meili, "Neun Thesen und eine persönliche Nachbemerkung zum Entwurf für das Klanghaus Toggenburg," in Hochbauamt des Kantons St.Gallen, Amt für Kultur, Kanton St.Gallen, *Klanghaus Toggenburg. Thesenkonkurrenz/Thesis Competition. Bericht des Preisgerichts/Report of the Jury*, 2010, Epilogue, p. 34, here p. 27.

16 Ibid.

The music is the emotional key that made the project acceptable to the majority

In 2012, Roth relinquishes the position of Artistic Director of the Klangwelt to the yodeler and artist Nadja Räss. Her contract includes the future role of Intendant of the Klanghaus. According to the artist and teacher, this was an opportunity to immerse herself in the culture of Ober-toggenburg. She still speaks enthusiastically about the challenge: "I was able to directly inherit the passion and fire that Peter Roth had brought to the role."[17] She calls the project an investment in our yodeling culture. Music is the connecting element across many boundaries, and it is also music that finally brings people together to support the Klanghaus. Räss adds that Roth is a source of ideas par excellence, whose projects can also be a challenge for the participants and all others involved. Her objective is to make the Klangwelt and its components tangible, including for the local population.

At the first public presentation of the building project by Meili in Wildhaus in 2012, the people of the village cite a number of arguments against the Klanghaus. Räss is present. She strikes up a Toggenburg yodel and the locals joined in. Thereafter, it is possible to discuss the Klanghaus in a new light. Räss says that it is essential that the people of Toggenburg support the Klanghaus and that it must also be their building. "The music is the emotional key that made the project acceptable to the majority," says Hilber.[18]

Failure as an opportunity

In 2014, the Mayor of Lichtensteig, Mathias Müller, becomes President of the Klangwelt Foundation. His role is to ensure that the project gains support across the region. When it fails to earn the approval of the Cantonal Parliament in 2016 by a mere four votes, Roth, Müller, Räss, and their fellow campaigners roll up their sleeves. Looking back, Hilber, who had passed on her role to her successor Martin Klöti in 2012, is certain that "these stumbling blocks were vital because they set something in motion."[19] A taskforce is set up to investigate the reasons for parliament's rejection.

Müller now says that this failure was an opportunity. "We analyzed the project once more, partly with the aim of increasing value creation for the local region. The Klanghaus requires the corresponding environment, a Klangcampus, a range of attractions that, for example, facilitates a different form of tourism—tourism that operates all year round."[20] Müller and other actors initiate a participative process in the local municipalities; there are workshops with experts from the fields of music, tourism, architecture, and regional development. He says that the discussions generated some good ideas. A working group is established

17 Conversation with Nadja Räss on August 26, 2024.

18 Conversation with Kathrin Hilber on July 23, 2024.

19 Conversation with Mathias Müller on July 10, 2024.

20 Ibid.

with representatives from the region, the Toggenburg Tourist Board, private individuals, and foundations—at times, over 200 people are involved. The project was, and remains, the work of many.

On December 6, 2016, a petition containing 10,000 signatures supporting the Klanghaus is handed over to the government. Roth and Klöti manage to raise 5.3 million Swiss Francs to cover the operation costs of the building for the first twenty years. The valley also provides support. An operational and financing concept is drawn up. Müller calls this concept Klanghaus 2.0. The revised project is submitted in 2018. "The decisive factor for the canton was this ability to cover the operating costs for twenty years," says Martin Klöti.[21] In the run-up to the referendum in 2019, Roth, Müller, the President of the Tourist Board, Max Nadig, and other supporters organize flash mobs featuring traditional music with performances from alphorn players and cowbell ringers. The general public of St.Gallen experiences the acoustic richness of the region at first hand.

Klöti, who lived and worked in Toggenburg for fourteen years, describes the Klanghaus as "an essentially social project."[22] He has helped to inform people about it in his role as a Cantonal Councilor. It is vital to share information so that such projects can gain support. "Music brings together people with different backgrounds, singing connects cultures. The Klanghaus is a project of social exchange, between country and city, young and old, Switzerland and the world," explains Klöti.[23] The notion of the Klangregion emerges, together with the slogan "Toggenburg Resounds."

The Klanghaus is a project of social exchange

The Klanghaus 2.0 concept is presented to the government a year after the rejection by parliament and is accepted by the Cantonal Council in 2019. Meili is seriously ill. Peter Roth sends him a text at 3 a.m. on March 18, 2019: "We're going to build the Klanghaus." The architect dies the same night.

Soon after this, the electors of St.Gallen vote for the Klanghaus on the Schwendisee. In Alt St. Johann, seventy-two percent are in favor of the project. Roth is still emotional today when he speaks about this verdict. It means a lot to him that the people of Obertoggenburg support the Klanghaus.

Marcel Meili started with the music and made the language his own

According to co-architect Astrid Staufer, Meili carried the Klanghaus on his shoulders. He was an intellectual who had the ability to inspire. It was impressive to experience

21 Conversation with Martin Klöti on August 6, 2024.

22 Ibid.

23 Ibid.

Fig. 3

Fig. 3
In the run-up to the referendum in 2019, Peter Roth, Mathias Müller, the President of the Tourist Board, Max Nadig, and other supporters organize flash mobs featuring traditional music with performances from alphorn players and cowbell ringers.

the way in which he threw himself into traditional music and Alpine culture. Hilber describes Meili's approach succinctly: "He started with the music and made the language his own."[24]

Staufer hopes that this spirit of sounding out and testing will continue amongst the musicians who get together in the building, because it lives on this atmosphere of curiosity and this ability to engage, from this experimental and intercultural approach. In this spirit, the building will be embedded in the Klangcampus, which is the overall concept for the area around the Klanghaus and includes, as its central component, the Resonanzzentrum Peter Roth—which will be discussed elsewhere. Roth paints a picture: "We already have the church and now we need the village as well."[25] In other words, the story continues and will flourish further due to the people who talk to one another, sing together, yodel, play music, and are won over by the world of sound—on the Schwendisee and beyond.

24 Conversation with Kathrin Hilber on July 23, 2024.

25 Conversation with Peter Roth on August 12, 2024.

Figs. 4–6
Sound Spaces: interaction between the interior and the exterior.

Fig. 4

Fig. 5

Fig. 6

1973	Peter Roth returns to Toggenburg from studying music in Zurich and begins to compose.
1977	Roth starts to offer lectures and courses. The main subjects: the Pythagorean harmonic series, customs of Toggenburg, natural yodeling, and the Alpine blessing.
1993	The former Naturfreundehaus Seegütli on the Schwendisee is purchased by Seegütli AG and becomes a course center.
2002	Launch of the concert cycle "850 years of Alt St. Johann." Roth speaks with Peter Zumthor. The Canton of St.Gallen shows interest in the Klanghaus project.
2003	Founding of the Klangwelt.
	Opening of the first stage of the Klangweg.
2004	The first "Natural Voices" Klangfestival takes place with artists from around the globe.
2005 2006	Second and third stages of the Klangweg.
2007 2008	The Canton of St.Gallen approves the preliminary project for the "Klanghaus Toggenburg." The Klangwelt becomes one of the canton's five priorities for cultural funding. The design contract with Peter Zumthor is put out to open tender.
2009	The project falls through due to the opposition of the architects' professional body; establishment of the Klangwelt Toggenburg Foundation.
2010	Public tender procedure: Thesis Competition for the Klanghaus, which is won by Marcel Meili, Meili, Peter Architekten.
2012	Peter Roth hands over the artistic directorship of the Klangwelt to Nadja Räss. Public presentation of the construction project in Wildhaus.
2012 2013	Development of the construction project, Marcel Meili with Staufer & Hasler Architekten.
2016	The proposal for the Klanghaus is rejected in the Cantonal Parliament by a qualified majority; the Klanghaus Taskforce is established.
	December 6, presentation of the petition with 10,000 signatures supporting the Klanghaus to the Government.
2017	Submission of the revised concept Klanghaus 2.0. Peter Roth and Martin Klöti raise 5.3 million francs for the operation costs of the Klanghaus.
2018	The project is endorsed by the Cantonal Parliament. The construction dispatch is approved.
2019	Marcel Meili dies on March 18. On June 30, the electors express their support for the Klanghaus. In Wildhaus Alt St. Johann, 71.1 percent vote for the project.
	Further development of the project by Staufer & Hasler Architekten and the project team.
2022	Start of construction.
2025	Opening of the Klanhaus.

In Search of Resonance. Toggenburg on the Path to Soft Tourism

Christian Gressbach

Located in the heart of Eastern Switzerland, between the striking peaks of Säntis and the Churfirsten, the region of Toggenburg is notable for its deep cultural roots and a quest for continuity. This is a place where people live in harmony with nature and with their customs. But present-day Toggenburg, like so many rural regions, faces the challenge of finding a balance between nurturing a cultural identity that has evolved over centuries and developing a sustainable economic base that does justice to this tradition.

This is the background to the question of how one of the most important cornerstones of the regional economy, tourism in Obertoggenburg, can be structured in such a way that it develops in harmony with, rather than reshapes, the landscape and the culture. The answer to this question seems to lie in the sounds that have characterized the valley for centuries and are now being heard in the Klanghaus Toggenburg, and which also have the potential not only to support tourism but also to cultivate the cultural identity and, hence, safeguard the future of the region. The search for a new way of traveling is reflected in the concept of resonance tourism, an idea that follows in the steps of soft tourism and sustainable tourism. The sociologist Hartmut Rosa describes resonance as a form of relationship with the world that is characterized not by availability and control but, rather, by openness and mindfulness. The trend was described as a potential future way of traveling in 2019.[1] In the same year, it was incorporated into Toggenburg's tourism strategy for 2025, which was also drawn up in view of the opening of the Klanghaus.[2]

1 Zukunftsinstitut, "Trendforschung" (www.zukunftsinstitut.de).

2 "Toggenburg Tourismus Strategie 2025," Toggenburg, 2021 (https://toggenburg.swiss/files/toggenburg.org/PDF/Toggenburg_Tourismus_Strategie_2025.pdf).

The eventful history of Toggenburg

But how did sound, which has long been part of local tradition, become the leitmotif of the destination and, hence, the basis for a new tourism model? The history of Toggenburg is one of change and religious tolerance.

This tolerance emerged out of the shared struggle against natural adversity and has been consolidated by the coexistence of the Evangelical and Catholic populations.

Toggenburg began to make a name for itself back in the early nineteenth century due to its indigenous textile industry. The impact of the production of the Toggenburger Tüechli[3] was felt throughout the valley. Numerous large weaving and spinning mills in Central and Lower Thurtal, the Heberlein yarn dyehouse in Wattwil, and hundreds of small suppliers in the field of cotton processing formed the industrial backbone of the region and employed over half of the people of Toggenburg. Since there were only a few factories, working at home played an important role: many farms combined small-scale agricultural activities with the weaving of fabric in the farm buildings. This form of labor supported the sense of independence of the local people and enabled them to organize their work flexibly. However, the textile sector was volatile. After 1860, the color-weaving industry began to shrink. Within just a few years, it had been replaced by the emerging embroidery industry. This then entered a period of crisis after the First World War as chemical dyeing and textile finishing grew in importance. At the same time, Central Toggenburg witnessed the growth of the machinery industry and, from the 1960s, the development of numerous small and medium-sized companies that produced high-precision instruments, plastics, and products that were used in food processing and cosmetics production.

In the midst of this industrial transformation, the foundations for tourism were laid. The same individuals who, in 1863, founded the Toggenburger Bank—which went on to develop into UBS—also laid the cornerstones for the construction of the Toggenburg Railway from Wil to Ebnat in 1870. This line, which was extended to Nesslau in 1912, the construction of the railway from Lake Constance to Toggenburg, and the expansion of the road network around the Churfirsten and the Alpstein opened up opportunities for the development of tourism.

The beginnings and heyday of tourism

The first summer tourism developed in Central and Upper Toggenburg after 1860 in the form of mountain resorts with healthy air and simple accommodation. Ski tourism followed in 1905 with skis that were initially produced locally. The area around the Churfirsten was particularly suitable for ski tours. The construction of the first funicular from Unterwasser to Iltios in 1934 and the subsequent opening up of Upper and Central Toggenburg were accompanied by investment in upscale hotels, while the simple pensions disappeared. Winter tourism expanded, with most guests coming from the region between Winterthur and St.Gallen. Notable events included the visits from

3 A highly versatile product of the color-weaving industry that can be used as a handkerchief or neckerchief and is part of the traditional costume of the region, the *Sennentracht*.

Queen Wilhelmina of the Netherlands and her daughter to Unterwasser, where they spent four weeks enjoying the sport and taking the air in both 1934 and 1935. After the Second World War, winter tourism flourished further and the region had over eighty funiculars and drag, ski, and chair lifts.[4] In contrast, the almost snow-free winters of the late 1980s triggered an enduring crisis in the tourism sector, and this necessitated a change of direction. Today, the focus is on all-year-round tourism and the question of how the region can be positioned as a complete destination without endangering the character of the valley and the everyday culture that has been fostered to date. The Klanghaus and the strategy of resonance tourism could provide an answer.

A region of modest tones

Toggenburg was and remains a region of soft tones, and this is reflected in its culture. The people here have a special relationship with nature and with their musical traditions, such as yodeling and choral singing. These traditions are an expression of the way in which the community is deeply rooted in the extraordinary landscape and of the development of this community over time. In around 1820, the Toggenburg priest Johannes Franz from Mogelsberg (1755–1855) was already waxing lyrical about the people of the region and their love of and talent for music, which was also apparent to the travelers who visited the local inns.[5] The German author Ludwig Bechstein (1810–1860), who was well known for his collections of German folktales and sagas, also reported enthusiastically upon his encounter with this world of sounds in a natural setting, where “the evening songs of the jaunty herdsmen and the penetrating tones of their whooping, which resembled a *Kuhreihen*, echoed around and below us from the Alps on every side, as they enticed their herds to gather for milking.”[6] This culture continues to this day and is now less a spectacle for outsiders than an intimate aspect of daily life that is part of the identity of the local people. It is precisely this modesty and reserve that lend the valley its charm—and, at the same time, represent a major challenge for the development of tourism. How can one market authenticity without distorting it?

Resonance tourism places the emphasis on sustainable experience by focusing on relationships: between visitors and locals, people and nature, past and present. The Klanghaus Toggenburg embodies this idea. It is not just an accessible instrument for musicians or choirs, but also a place of encounter and exchange, a space for resonance. This is a venue where visitors can immerse themselves in the Klangwelt (Sound World) of Toggenburg, in the music, the landscape, and the culture. The concept of the building is based on the idea that sound is a universal language that connects people, regardless of their origins

4 Toggenburg, in *Historisches Lexikon der Schweiz HSL*, version of March 16, 2017.

5 “Because, when a visitor to Wildhaus encounters a group of around twenty young people, he can be sure that twelve or fourteen of them will be musical, some will play the violin, others will reveal themselves to be good singers, some will play the organ, others the zither, and several the clarinet, while others blow the bassoon, as a result of which they’ll be able to put on a wonderful concert.” Büchler, Hans, “Das oberste Toggenburg um 1820,” in *200 Jahre Zwinglianische Gesellschaft Wildhaus-Alt St. Johann*, Schwellbrunn, 2024, pp. 17–48, trans. by R.H.

6 Ibid., pp. 38–40, trans. by R.H. A *Kuhreihen* is a melody played by herdsmen as they accompany cattle in the Swiss Alps.

and experience. This connection creates resonance—in both the individual and the collective sense.

An offer for the region and for its visitors

In the past few decades, Toggenburg has developed a full range of options for tourists related to the subject of sound. The Klangwelt Toggenburg, which was initiated by Peter Roth in 2001, was the starting point. The development of the interactive Klangweg (Sound Trail), the Klangfestival (Sound Festival), and the Klangschmiede (Sound Smith) has created a tourist infrastructure that ties in with the culture of the region to facilitate special and singular encounters with sound and nature. This is an approach based on the quality and holistic nature of the experience. But even if such an offering seems ideal in terms of sustainable tourism, there still remains the question of whether it can fulfill the associated economic requirements. The infrastructure and facilities have to be maintained and the people who work for the Klangwelt have to be paid. The Klanghaus Toggenburg offers an experience that is independent of the season or the weather, geared towards group and educational programs, and focused on the encouragement of overnight stays rather than day trips. But even soft tourism must reach a certain scale if it is to be economically viable over the long term. In this context, the Klanghaus is an attempt to find a balance between economic viability and the sensitive use of our ecological and cultural resources. It is a conscious alternative approach in a competitive market that is often dominated by mass offerings and rapid growth. It offers experiences that resist the normal mechanisms of tourism.

A genuine "we culture"

The resonance generated by this process goes beyond sound and the Klanghaus as a cultural institution. It concerns the entire region and is changing the way in which tourism is seen and practiced. The Klangcampus project that has evolved out of the Klanghaus demonstrates the depth of the changes that are envisaged here. A network of actors is working to offer holistic experiences to visitors to the region. The intention is that the area known as Schwendi above the villages of Wildhaus and Unterwasser will combine with the Klanghaus to form a resort that is focused on encounters.

A central element of this network is the cooperation between the Klangwelt, the hotels, pensions, and restaurants, the cable-car operators, and the tourist organizations. The common goal of the service providers and the people of Schwendi is that all development around the Klanghaus—whether touristic, cultural, architectural, economic, or agricultural—is sustainable, circumspect, and soft.
 Plans and projects are shared, interests and ideas are jointly

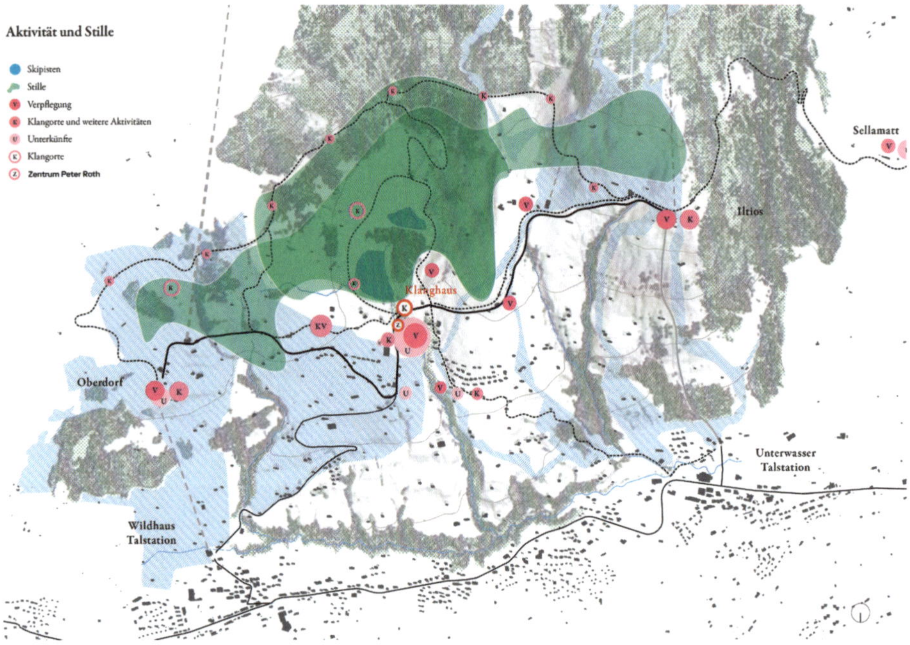

Fig. 1

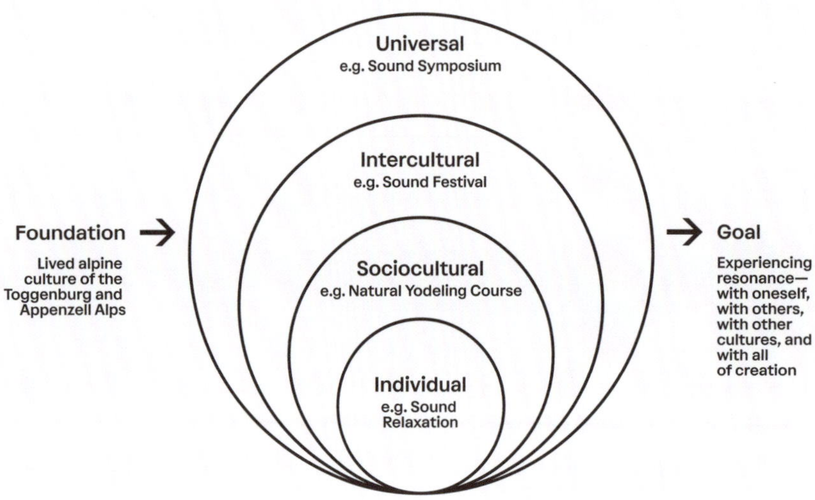

Fig. 2

Fig. 3

Fig. 1
"Activity and Calm," from: Herzog & de Meuron and Studio Noun, Study for the Klangcampus site. Territorial development concept and architectural guidelines, 2021/22 (updated for this publication).

Fig. 2
Peter Roth, Resonance model, 2019.

Fig. 3
Panoramic map of the Klangcampus, summer; from: Herzog & de Meuron and Studio Noun, Study for the Klangcampus site. Territorial development concept and architectural guidelines, 2021/22 (updated for this publication).

discussed, and synergies are exploited and coordinated in a respectful manner. One manifestation of this network is the cooperation between locals, tourism professionals, and artists, which is based on mutual appreciation. The architectural embodiment of this culture is the Resonanzzentrum Peter Roth, which will serve as the reception building for the Klangcampus from May 2025. This center, which is situated just 200 meters below the Klanghaus, supports the notion of the platform economy, whereby the value created by tourism is shared and a range of stakeholders are actively involved. The Klanghaus and the Resonanzzentrum act as meeting places that not only provide an economic stimulus for the region, but also facilitate a new way of looking at tourism and culture—as a genuine "we culture," which is able to successfully combine innovation, tradition, and sustainability.

The tranquility of Toggenburg, which is brought into focus by the Klanghaus, is not only an acoustic phenomenon but also a symbol for the inner calm that many visitors come here to find. It is a place for slowing down in an ever-more hectic world, a place in which one can resonate—with oneself, with other people and cultures, with the universe. It is this resonance that differentiates Toggenburg from other destinations. The sound that rings out here is more than just a tourist attraction: it is firmly anchored in the culture and day-to-day life of the people of Toggenburg and, at the same time, an expression of a profound search for a new way of traveling. The Klanghaus also embodies the hopes and longings of a region that is seeking stability and depth in a fast-changing world.

The text emerged from fruitful conversations with the historian Hans Büchler, a specialist in the local history of Toggenburg.

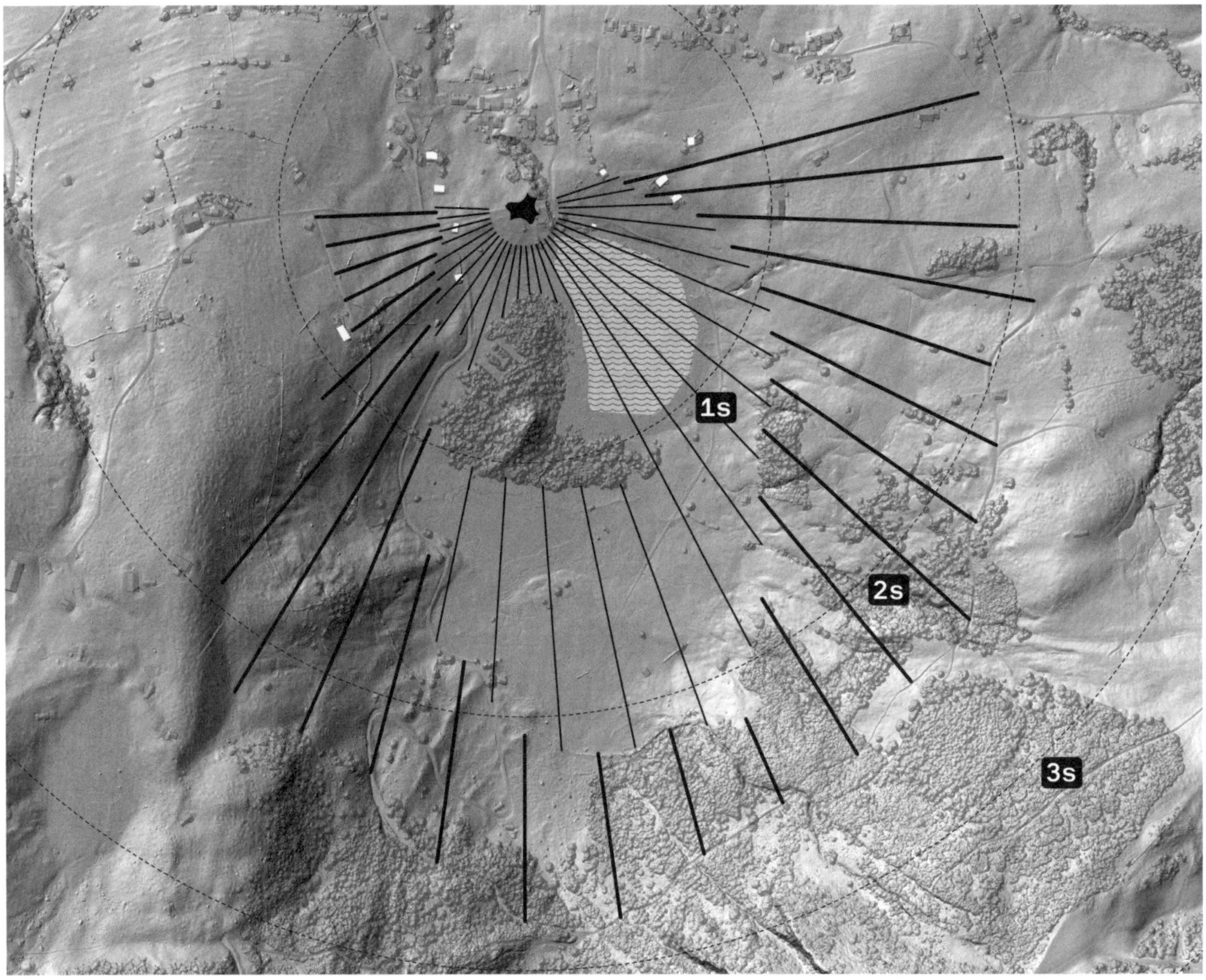

An echo star for the immediate surroundings of the Klanghaus: A call from the external stage in the direction of Schwendisee is answered from a number of echo points in the illustrated subdivisions of the landscape. The visualized sound paths work in both directions, the call multiplies, and the echo returns with precision from each stimulated echo point to the point of origin. We hear the phono-topology over the Schwendisee. (Andres Bosshard)

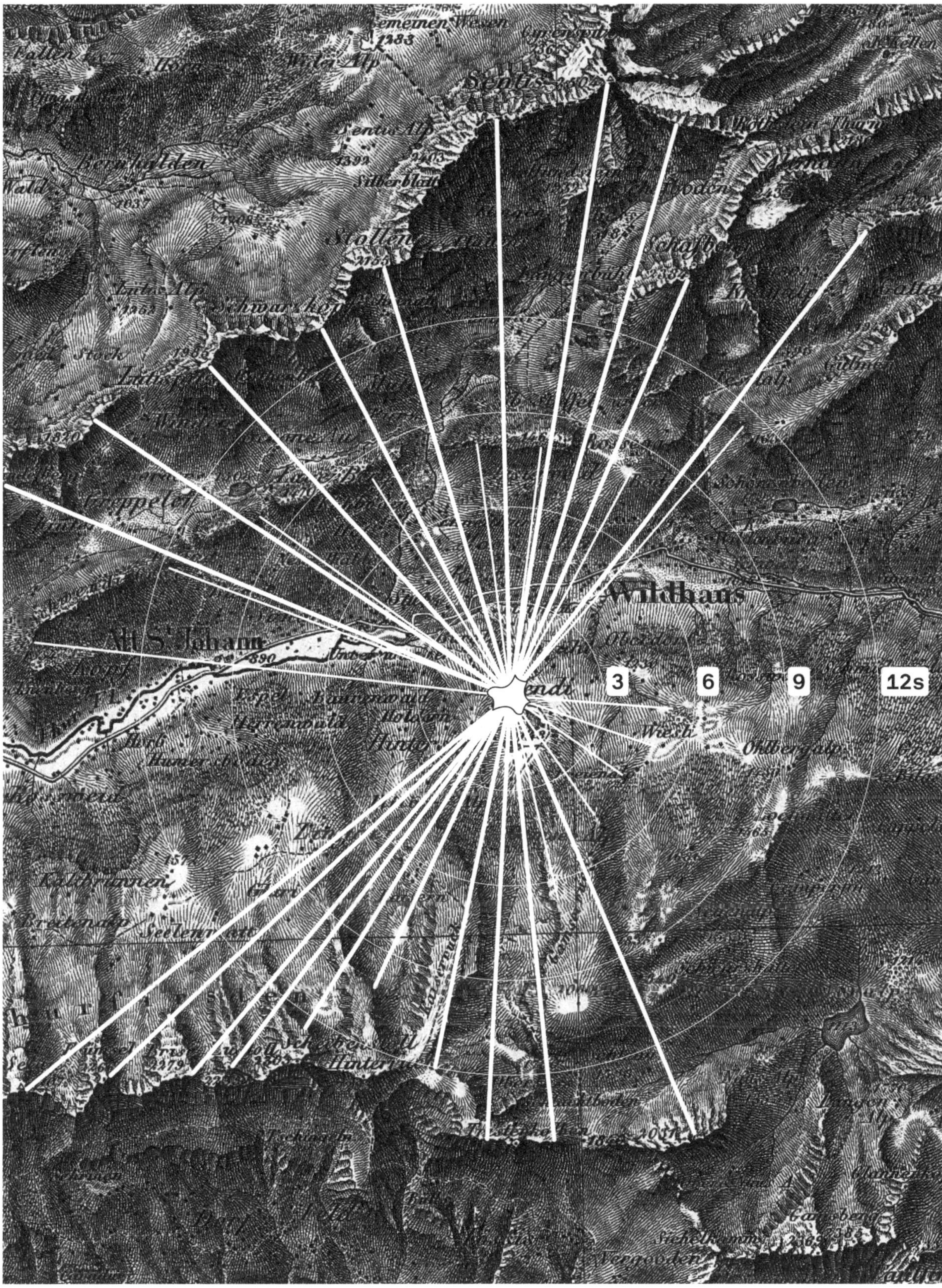

An echo star for Upper Toggenburg with the Klanghaus at its center: The semicircle of steep rock faces of the Säntiskette to the north and the mountainous flanks of the Churfirsten to the south form a broad, high-altitude arena. The sound paths are easy to identify in summer storms or as helicopters fly by. Twenty-three bronze acoustic mirrors in the central space of the Klanghaus form a precise and clearly audible model of this Toggenburg phono-topology. (Andres Bosshard)

Songs from the Heart. Ulrich Bräker's Acoustic Worlds

Alfred Messerli

Ulrich Bräker was born as a farmer's son in Toggenburg in 1735, and went on to become a small-scale merchant. The autodidact, whose autobiography *Lebensgeschichte und Natürliche Ebentheuer des Armen Mannes im Tockenburg*[1] brought him fame across Europe upon its publication in 1798, lived his life embracing and rejecting the major influential trends of the century, within both reformed confessions such as orthodoxy and Pietism and the intellectual movement of the Enlightenment. Pietism in particular, which had been demanding personal devotion, the individual experience of faith, and a vibrant religiousness as a reaction to Reformed orthodoxy since the final quarter of the seventeenth century, set the tone in the poor farming family in which Bräker grew up and also shaped his initial relationship with folkloristic singing.

The more than 3,000 pages of his diaries, which cover the period between 1768 and 1798, his autobiography, which was published as a book in 1789, his two plays, and his other writings provide a rich vein of material about songs and singing. Bräker listened to songs being sung, wrote his own, sang songs, reflected on singing and lyrics, and, finally, collected songs, which he recorded in a slender songbook entitled *vermischte lieder vor den land-mann. oder poetische phantaseyen eines ungepflantzten, wild-gewachsenen dichters. gesrieben in toggenburgschen gebirgen: 1779.*[2]

As a boy, Bräker herded goats; he started with thirty and, after three years, had more than one hundred. He considered that one of the "joys of the herdsman's role" was the opportunity to sing with the birds: "Oh! What did I feel then!—Ah, I know not! Stay sweet, sweet bliss! Then I'd sing and trill with them till I got hoarse."[3] And when Bräker, as a twenty-year-old Prussian soldier, visited Schottmann's cellar in Berlin with his friend Schärer after exercises to drink a beer and smoke a pipe, they sang a "Swiss song": "The Brandenburgers and Pomeranians there always loved

1 Translated by Derek Bowman and published in English as *Ulrich Bräker, The Life Story and Real Adventures of the Poor Man of Toggenburg*, Edinburgh, 1970.

2 See Ulrich Bräker, *Sämtliche Schriften in 5 Bänden*, bearbeitet von Andreas Bürgi, Alfred Messerli et al., 5 vols., vol. IV, Munich, 2000, pp. 76–122; vol. V, Munich, 2000, pp. 702–12 (commentary).

3 Bräker 1970, p. 27.

Fig. 1
First page of Ulrich Bräker's *vermischte lieder vor den land-mann*, 1779.

vermischte lieder
vor den land=mann.
oder
poetische phantaseyen
eines ungepflantzten, wildgewachsenen dichters.
gesrieben in toggenburgschen gebirgen:
1779 ||

wie mancher gute baur –
der auf seim gütchen lebet,
seingt holops auf der flur;
wan sich sein hertz erhebet.
er seingt nach eigner weis,
die offt kein herr versteht;
er fragt nicht glehrten fleiß,
wils ihm von hertzen geht. ||

Michel zum sohn; im mertz.

he, lustig bub, der frühling kommt;
s'hat mir die nacht von kirschen traumt,
heür gibts ein gutes jahr;
glaubs bub, ich merks den vögeln an;
wirst sehen was der äty kan;
treügts mich, bin ich ein narr.

nur frisch und munter, seing u. pfeif,
die betzger von den hosen streif:
wir gehen morn ins feld:
wend scheinden, brennen haber=sään,
und dann zum bohnen aker gehn
die arbeit macht ein held. ||

heür grathet alles was mann pflanzt,
das mann im herbst vor freüde tanzt,

to listen to us. Some gentlemen would even send for us to come over to a cook-shop, specially to sing the *Kuhreihen* (shepherd's song) to them; usually payment consisted of nothing but a portion of fatty soup; but in such straits you're glad of even less."[4] This is an example of the *Kuhreihen* becoming an early folkloristic happening in a major European city. Bräker's recollection is not free of comic irony, given the theory, which was widely shared in the eighteenth century, that Swiss soldiers who sang a *Kuhreihen* while serving abroad risked receiving the death penalty. In 1798, Johann Gottfried Ebel reported this as follows: "If *Kuhreihen* were played or sung by Swiss regiments serving in France, the sons of the Alps melted into tears and suddenly succumbed to homelessness of such epidemic proportions that, if they were unable to return to the fatherland, they would desert or die. This extraordinary effect of that Alpine music was the reason why either singing or whistling the *Kuhreihen* was prohibited on pain of death."[5] There was, however, no truth to this story of the death penalty.

This basic pietistic disposition of the young Ulrich Bräker oscillated between the jubilant celebration of God's creation on one side and a cautious observation of his own behavior on the other. The constant aim was to avoid sinning so that one would not miss out on the chance of future salvation. And almost everything was sinful. In a warning "to myself and my family" dating from 1768[6]—he was thirty-four years old at the time and four of his seven children had already been born—he speaks of how "the Lord's Sabbath is horribly" defiled by the fact that countless sins are committed, more than on weekdays, in "inns, with their disgraceful talking, bawdy singing, joking, swearing, laughing, fighting, arguing, and mocking of the devout."[7] Conversely, nine years later, a dialogue in Bräker's diary entitled, "gespräche Rudolf Suter Priest of Wattweil—die neüe und alte pfarrwahl,"[8] reports how a certain Wäspi rails against the "mean reforming" of Father Lavater of Zurich, who wanted to forbid his countrymen from singing on New Year's Eve. Rather, he "[gave] twice as much as usual to all those who came to my window and sang about the ban. I was often on the verge of shedding tears—about the fact that that preposterous priest had banned the merry singers from our windows—in a season that is full of joy—the dozy fool."[9]

In 1780, Bräker reported how, two evenings earlier, he had traveled with two friends to Schwellbrunn (AR): "there was a gathering there of women and men—girls and boys; a bunch of jolly folk from Appenzell, who had come from Urnäsch for the parish fair." Bräker was particularly impressed by the "boys and girls": "Upon my soul—such uniquely remarkable fellows—the boys whooped for all they were worth, and then sang *Kuhreihen* splendidly: Only someone bereft of feelings could have failed to be shaken

4 Ibid., p. 125.

5 Johann Gottfried Ebel, *Schilderung der Gebirgsvölker der Schweiz*, 2 vols. Leipzig, 1798, 1802, vol. 1, p. 418, transl. by R.H.

6 See Bräker, *Sämtliche Schriften*, vol. 1, Munich, 1998, pp. 1–118.

7 Ibid., p. 34, transl. by R.H.

8 Bräker, *Sämtliche Schriften*, vol. 2, Munich, 1998, pp. 299–321 (August 25, 1782), transl. by R.H.

9 Ibid., p. 303.

Fig. 2

Fig. 2
Franz Niklaus, Josef Reinhard, *Ulrich und Salome Bräker*, vernis mou, around 1801.

to the core—by songs that were not the slightest bit crude—or could have reacted negatively to the fine voices—with their soothing, inimitable tone—whether it was dishonorable for me to do so or not—I listened to them with inner pleasure—and believe—that even the best concert could not have delighted me so much."[10] We know from Johann Rudolf Steinmüller's *Beschreibung der schweizerischen Alpen- und Landwirthschaft* (1804) that the cows were called together on the alpine pastures by the wordless chanting of the herders, "which the people of Appenzell call *löcklen* (which comes from *lokken*, lure) or *zauren* or *zorren* (whooping); or *rugusen* or *rugüslen* (natural yodeling)."[11] "The female inhabitants of Innerrhoden are particularly" adept at this "and are able to practice this skill—from eight to nine-year-old girls to fifty and sixty-year-old women—as a way of mustering the cows from the greatest of distances, in the middle of the day, whenever they desire."[12] And while this wordless melody of the "*Löcklen* or *Rugusen*" summons the cows to the cowshed, the herdsman only sings the *Kuhreihen* (a lyrical yodel) "when he ties the cows up in the stall or milks them, one after the other—in a row or *Reihe*,—or as he leads the cows as they climb to their mountain pastures or descend to the valley."[13] Things will have been much the same in Toggenburg.

Steinmüller concludes by reporting, like Bräker before him, about a process that can be understood as a form of aestheticisation—and that is not dissimilar to the process of folklorization identified above. The erstwhile working songs of the herders are now objects of pastime and pleasure: "Furthermore, every member of an Appenzell dance troupe must also be able to play the *Kuhreihen* on their violin—in a danceable way, as the herdsman says—and it is also currently common practice in *Appenzell Innerrhoden* for the young people to dance every year to the *Kuhreihen*—in their *Alpstubeten* (alpine parlors) up in the pastures below an open sky and down in the valley during carnival."[14]

10 Ibid., pp. 210–11 (August 16, 1780), transl. by R.H.; see also Bräker, *Sämtliche Schriften*, vol. 3, Munich, 1998, p. 128 (April 20, 1789).

11 Johann Rudolf Steinmüller, Beschreibung der schweizerischen Alpen- und Landwirthschaft, nach den verschiedenen Abweichungen einzelner Kantone, 2 vols, vol. 2, Winterthur, 1804, p. 125, transl. by R.H.

12 Ibid., pp. 127–28.

13 Ibid., pp. 128–29.

14 Ibid., pp. 129.

Ulrich Bräker possibly sung very little in his later years; but he liked to listen when others were singing, and he also wrote his own songs, gathered information about songs, and documented those that were unknown to him. For example, he noted down a satirical song directed at the Catholic pilgrims from Southern Germany who passed through the region: "poor pilgrims, what are you carrying home; empty bags and tired legs."[15] While journeying on foot to Zurich (a week after the storming of the Bastille in Paris) he listened to "the singing reapers with heartfelt delight."[16] In the days preceding the creation of the Helvetic Republic (1798–1803) there was a revolution in Wattwil, the main town in Toggenburg.[17] And Ulrich Bräker reports how the people elected their representatives; there was "music—and joyful singing rang out—people moved around in processions, dancing and singing songs of freedom."[18]

15 Bräker, *Sämtliche Schriften*, vol. 2, Munich, 1998, p. 484 (October 4, 1784), transl. by R.H.

16 Bräker, *Sämtliche Schriften*, vol. 3, Munich, 1998, p. 199 (July 21, 1789), transl. by R.H.

17 See Bräker, *Sämtliche Schriften*, vol. 3, Munich, 1998, pp. 716–19 (February 1798): "jm hornung—revolution im Toggenburg."

18 Ibid., p. 717.

Fig. 3

Fig. 4

Fig. 5

Fig. 6

Fig. 7

Fig. 8

The Klangweg Toggenburg (Sound Trail Toggenburg) consists of twenty-seven sound sculptures, which can be investigated and listened to by visitors. There is a focus on subjects such as nature, the sound-sphere, sound ecology, climate, or mindfulness.

Fig. 3
Klangwelt, *Bet(t)ruftrichter*, 2024.

Fig. 4
Walter Hadorn, *Brunnen-stubete*, 2006/2021.

Fig. 5
René Düsel, *Glockenbühne*, 2005.

Fig. 6
Marco Barotti, *Woodpeckers*, 2024.

Fig. 7
Frédéric Laffont, *The Ringing and Shining Flowers*, 2024.

Fig. 8
View of the Klanghaus and Schwendisee, 2024.

In Harmony with Nature. Some Thoughts on Natural Yodeling

Lea Hagmann with Sonja Lieberherr-Schnyder

"Sometimes, when I'm up here on the Neuenalp and all the cows are wearing their bells, I suddenly have the impression that someone is yodeling! A melody emerges from the sound of the bells."[1] Matthias Huser is a dairy farmer and cheesemaker. As the son of the Obertoggenburg natural yodeler Annelies Huser-Ammann, he grew up listening to the sound of his mother yodeling. Although he has never sung in a yodeling choir, these melodies are buried deep within him, are part of his world. "This sound was there long before I was born. And it will also remain here far longer than we do."

Natural yodeling is a special way of singing: not with words as in yodel songs, but with different syllables, the switching of registers between the head and the chest. As someone who didn't grow up with yodeling, I think of choirs of men wearing traditional costume, some singing solos while the others accompany them with a flat chord. Such rudimentary ideas accompany me as I join the Toggenburg natural yodeler Sonja Lieberherr-Schnyder on a visit to the yodelers Annelies Huser-Ammann from Alt St. Johann and Christian Metzler from Nesslau. Both have been involved for many years with their local yodeling choirs, the Churfirstenchörli and Jodlerklub Männertreu, respectively.

As an ethnomusicologist, I am well aware that my role is not to write *about* people and their music but, rather, to listen to them, to try and understand *their* perspectives and ideas, and to describe these with the help of specialist concepts and models. In ethnomusicology, this method is known as "Grounded Theory,"[2] and the insider perspective of these bearers of our culture is referred to by the technical term "emic" and contrasts with the external—the "etic"—perspective.[3] In order to be able to represent both of these approaches, Sonja and I have teamed up—she as an insider and I as an outsider. Together, we want to discover how the people of Toggenburg talk about natural

1 The interview with Annelies Huser and Matthias Huser was conducted by Sonja Lieberherr-Schnyder and Lea Hagmann in Alt St. Johann, July 10, 2024.

2 Barney G. Glaser and Anselm L. Strauss, *Grounded Theory. Strategien qualitativer Forschung*, Bern, 2005.

3 Thomas Krefeld, "Die 'emische' und die 'etische' Forschungsperspektive," in *Lehre in den Digital Humanities*, 2020.

Fig. 1
Nesselhalde, Halden, and Burst with Mittelberg in the background.

Fig. 1

yodeling and to learn what connects them with yodeling and why they regard it as more than just a style of singing.

Inspired by the acoustic landscape

"When we sat on the hay cart as kids and heard the motor humming, the tone was like an accompaniment for us. We sang and yodeled against the background of the engine noise," recalls Annelies Huser. For her, natural yodeling emerges directly from the surrounding sounds. "These can be any sounds: bells, the wind whistling around your hat, or even the milking machine. You suddenly hear melodies emerging from these everyday sounds and you begin to hum along and then, if you feel like it, you yodel." With a cheeky smile, she adds: "In the milking parlor, where all the milk churns are hanging, it sounds particularly good."

Christian Metzler was also brought up with natural yodeling from an early age: "As a boy, I always yodeled while feeding the cows in the stall at home. And during haymaking. I first arranged the hay in strips (so-called *Heumaden*) with the fork and then I jumped up onto the blower, which distributed the hay. Up there, I yodeled as loud as I could while the motor chugged along providing the bass line."[4]

The scenes described to us here by Metzler and Huser distinctly overlap with the concept of "Soundscapes" coined by the Canadian acoustic researcher R. Murray Schafer in the 1970s.[5] For Schafer, every sound that we encounter in our daily lives is part of a composition. We are also partly responsible for this composition, because we complement such sounds of nature as the ripple of a stream, the murmuring of the forest, or the roaring of the storm by adding some sounds of our own, whether sung or spoken, imitations of nature, or the human built environment, the sounds of bells or engines.

4 The interview with Christian Metzler was conducted by Sonja Lieberherr-Schnyder and Lea Hagmann in Nesslau on July 10, 2024.

5 R. Murray Schafer, *The Soundscape. Our Sonic Environment and the Tuning of the World*, Rochester, Vermont, 1993 [1977].

Fig. 2

Fig. 2
Säntis and Schafberg.

In other words, nourished by these acoustic landscapes, natural yodeling is far from being an isolated style of singing. Rather, it is closely connected with its surroundings. Huser's son Matthias, who joins us for a cup of coffee between working on the fields and the evening milking, describes it as follows: "For me, it all belongs together: yodeling, working up the mountain, the bells. All of this is my life."

Strengthening the sense of community

Yodeling is not only heard as people work. It also plays an important role in bringing people together socially—a process that ethnomusicology calls "Community Building"—and, thus, has a social function. "For me, the most wonderful experiences have always been in the taverns," says Matthias. "When one person starts up and the others join in. That has always touched me the most." His mother agrees: "I find the experience of yodeling with other people even better than yodeling alone. This togetherness, this merging."

This communal aspect is also central for Metzler. "I'm always telling young yodelers: It's important not to think that you're something exceptional. You are lucky and privileged to be the lead yodeler in a club, you have the good fortune—and the gift—to have a good voice and a good ear for music. Good harmony always requires everyone: the whole choir is always needed."

This parity between the lead yodelers and the choir is essential for Community Building. Huser extends the concept even further: "What happens is, you're only as important as the listeners. You shouldn't think that you're more important than your listeners. You're merely the one who sings or yodels."

The ethnomusicologist Christopher Small uses the term "musicking" to describe this phenomenon of an equal community of musicians and listeners as depicted by Huser and Metzler.[6] In contrast with Western classical music, traditional music is not a separate entity, but rather part of an activity that covers everything from composing to performing and listening, as well as integrating this music into everyday life.

6 Christopher G. Small, *Musicking. The Meanings of Performing and Listening*, Middletown, Connecticut, 1998.

At the same time, the perfect musical result plays a secondary role in this "musicking." In other words, for Huser, a trained and balanced voice is not a criterion for an authentic natural yodel: "It moves me when someone yodels and I get the feeling that as a child, this person has trod barefoot in a cowpat somewhere up the mountain—this muck, this growing-up in the whole context, this 'herdsmen' sound." She adds: "The voice doesn't need to be so clear at every level and can even stumble or drag a bit between registers." Metzler underlines this view: "Here in Toggenburg, we're strongly subject to historical and social developments, in singing, in natural yodeling, in everything. And there was a period when natural yodeling was interpreted in a classical music style as clear-cut, absolutely perfect, but this no longer has much to do with the traditional natural yodeling that moves us."

From everyday life onto the stage

When the Churfirstenchörli in Alt St. Johann, founded in 1984, was on the lookout for women members, the enthusiastic singer Annelies Huser did not hesitate to put herself forward. She joined the choir as one of only two women in 1986. In the choir, she became familiar with not only yodel songs, which had always also been sung by women, but also natural yodeling, a tradition that had previously been restricted to the men of Obertoggenburg: "The men go up the mountain and the men yodel. That was simply the culture up here," explains Huser. But her voice, which is as clear as a bell, also earns her huge respect from the men. When the choir gathered to sing upon arriving back in their home village from a visit to a yodeling festival, she was spontaneously prodded by a lead yodeler and told that she should sing the first voice, the lead yodel. This marked the start of her extraordinary yodeling career.

Christian Metzler's heyday as a lead yodeler began when he was sixteen. This was quite a feat alongside his school work, since being a member of a yodeling club means attending at least one practice a week, as well as the numerous performances. But for Metzler, life without yodeling would have been unthinkable. And his enormous talent, coupled with his great modesty, meant that it was not long before he was able to assume the role of lead yodeler—despite the fact that older lead yodelers do not always find it easy to make way for the next generation.

Modesty is also a quality that distinguishes Huser. The fact that natural yodeling has a place both on stage and in the church was something that she initially had to get used to. "First of all, I had to learn that people like to hear you yodeling. For me, it was simply part of my daily life. I only gradually became aware that it can really also give people pleasure." The fact that she also received a fee for performing in these concerts was such a surprise that Huser was initially almost unable to accept it: "I had a really bad conscience. I don't need to be paid for doing something that I love and that comes so naturally to me."

The phenomenon described here by Huser is known in ethnomusicology as "Decontextualization": a musical tradition that has a fixed role in everyday life is removed from its context and placed in a new one. In this case, natural yodeling is transferred from the mountainside to a concert stage with a paying audience.[7] The music suddenly has a monetary value, due to a process that researchers call "commodification."[8]

Hence, yodeling in everyday life and yodeling in a concert are two completely different scenarios. Huser describes this very vividly: "It's like having two lives: you go from this life into the other and then back again. When I'm wearing my traditional costume it's as if I've slipped into the role of another woman: 'Now I've got a performance, now I'm off to yodel!' But then I'm always happy to get home, to get away from the hustle and bustle and back to the peace and quiet. Because these concert performances also take a lot of energy. You expose yourself completely with your voice and you cannot hide."

More than a style of singing

Natural yodeling is a way of opening up emotionally that goes far beyond mere words. Rather than needing to be cognitively translated, the feelings emerge directly in the sound. This is why natural yodeling is suitable for both happy and sad occasions. Huser offers an example: "You can sing 'Wildhuser' at a baptism in the church, you can sing it at a wedding, you can sing it at a funeral, you can always sing it. It's always the same melody, but you can sing it slower, faster, with more reflection or more humor, and this means that you can vary it according to the occasion. It seems to me that this requires a certain sensitivity, a feeling for the music, for the mood, for the moment."

The ability of natural yodeling to help us deal with life's darkest moments was also experienced by Metzler when he lost his father to a tragic accident while working on the field: "I was the only person who was there. My little sister was just three months old, I was sixteen, and my oldest brother seventeen. Life had to go on. Yes, I yodeled a lot at the time. I've no idea if this was a way of dealing with my loss."

7 Juniper Hill and Caroline Bithell, "An Introduction to Music Revival as Concept, Cultural Process, and Medium of Change," in Caroline Bithell and Juniper Hill (eds.), *The Oxford Handbook of Music Revival*, Oxford and New York, 2014, pp. 3–42.

8 Timothy Taylor, "Music on the move, as object, as commodity," in J. R. McNeill and Kenneth Pomeranz (eds.), *The Cambridge World History*, vol. VII, part II "Shared Transformations?", Cambridge, 2015, pp. 205–224.

Fig. 3

Fig. 3
Silberplatten in the Alpstein massif.

The idea of using natural yodeling as vocal therapy has now also reached urban areas. This could be one reason why the need to explore natural yodeling is currently growing at such a rate and why the Klanghaus Toggenburg is likely to assume an important role here. At the same time, however, Sonja Lieberherr-Schnyder feels that it is essential for us to really understand the context in which natural yodeling developed and in which it is at home: "I believe that people today are longing for the very same thing that we up here in Toggenburg have always been lucky enough to have. And we don't even have words to describe this sense of connectedness because it's simply part of our being." Huser adds: "We grew up here with this tradition and all these customs and we know how valuable our culture is. That's why it's important that we look after it."

To me as an ethnomusicologist, something became very clear in the course of these conversations with local yodelers: natural yodeling cannot simply be learnt in a singing class; it has to be understood in its context. It is part of an entire cosmology and, as such, much more than just a style of singing. It emerges in direct dialogue with the acoustic landscape in which the yodeler finds themselves, it shapes communities, it is an expression of the greatest joy and the deepest sorrow, and it even works as a form of therapy for people dealing with serious misfortunes. "All those who feel the yodel have learnt yodeling as part of their everyday life," summarizes Metzler before contemplating for a while, and then adding: "Natural yodeling is actually praying without words."

Fig. 4

Fig. 4
Schwendisee.

Glossary: Natural Yodeling

Natural yodeling	• Form of yodeling that is sung without words using so-called "neutral" syllables
Regions	• Northeastern Switzerland (Toggenburg, Appenzell Innerrhoden, Appenzell Ausserrhoden) • Central Switzerland (Muotatal, Ob- and Nidwalden, Entlebuch) • Canton of Bern (Berner Oberland)
Names	• *Naturjodel, Johlen* (Toggenburg) • *Zäuerli, Zauren* (Appenzell Ausserrhoden) • *Ruggusse(r)li* (Appenzell Interrhoden) • *Juuz* (Muotatal) • *Juiz* (Ob- and Nidwalden) • *Jutz* (Entlebuch) • *Naturjutz* (Berner Oberland)
Voices	• *Lead yodeler / "vorjohle"*: the 1st voice, who begins the natural yodel as a solo • *Second voice / "noofahre"**: the 2nd voice, who follows the melody of the lead yodeler at an interval of a third or a sixth, usually above the 1st voice * Some yodelers describe the 2nd voice as "gradhäbe" (rather than as "noofahre"). Both varieties exist.[9] • *Choir / "gradhäbe"* (drone): the choir starts last and holds the accompanying chord
Accompanying chords	• *grad* — home key, tonic • *vercheert* — 5th degree, dominant • *hinderschi* — 4th degree, subdominant

9 Raymond Ammann, Andrea Kammermann, and Yannick Wey, *Jodeln im Kopf. Erkenntnisse einer musikkognitiven Untersuchung im Alpsteingebiet*, Zurich, 2021.

Looking beyond the horizon—a global perspective

Yodel-like forms of singing can be found all around the globe, although they differ widely in terms of their musical and conceptual contexts. What they all share is the fact that they require very few or even no words at all and, instead, employ so-called "neutral syllables"—syllables that are not loaded with semantic content. Some of these forms of yodeling, such as Georgian Krimanchuli*, resemble Swiss natural yodeling in that they involve a rapid change of registers; others such as the* Yeli *of the Central African Aka or the* Diyei *of the Cameroonian Baka (who were formerly known as "pygmies") only function as a form of interwoven, contrapuntal polyphony and are never heard in* a solo context. The Yoik *(which is also known as* Luohti or Vuelie) *of the Indigenous Sámi minority in Northern Scandinavia and on Russia's Kola Peninsula originally emerged from shamanism, and its melody and rhythm describe the essence or the soul of a person, an animal, or an important place in the landscape. Today, it is used as a form of sung protest against the repressive policies of the Scandinavians and the Russians. Other forms of non-semantic singing, often combined with drumming and dancing, also appear in many Native American cultures, and the best known of these is probably the* Powwow. *In contrast, the Swedish* Kulning *and Iranian* Khele *originate from herding practices and are used in the driving of cows, sheep, and goats. Such forms of calling animals are gradually disappearing in step with the modernization of agriculture. While there may be acoustic similarities between all these styles of singing, it is important, from an ethnomusicological perspective, that they are not all labeled as "yodeling" (at most "yodel-like singing"), and that each tradition is considered distinctly, and in its own right.*

The Material Vitality of Shingles. On Materiality, Handcraft, and Contrapuntal Transformation Processes

Susanna Koeberle

What is a tree? What is wood? What is heartwood? Or sapwood? What exactly is the phloem? And what do we mean by cambium? While most readers will be able to offer a rough answer to the first two questions, the other terms will be less familiar. However, materially, all these words mean the same thing: wood, in the broadest sense. But just as not all trees are the same, not all wood is the same. And if we zoom in even closer, we can clearly differentiate between the various parts of a tree trunk. The above-mentioned technical terms are far from being the only ones that enable us to describe this highly complex organic material more precisely. However, the first answer to the question of what the facade and the inner workings of the Klanghaus on the Schwendisee are made of is likely to be simply "wood." And that would be a correct, if imprecise, answer.

I will start at a relatively obvious visual level, because anyone approaching the Klanghaus notices the special structure of the facade. This is made of shingles, of a collection, or more precisely, an assemblage of wooden elements. I will return to assemblage later. These elements cover the entire exterior of the three-winged building like scales or a form of skin. Such a wooden skin of scales is not unusual per se, because there is a tradition of shingle facades in Toggenburg. And yet the building stands out, due not only to its unusual design, but also to the light tone of this shingle facade. Or at least it does for the moment. For these spruce shingles will soon change their color. On my second visit, just two months after my first, the areas of gently curving facade already looked different. Depending upon the orientation and the form of the roof, the wood was already discolored in some places. And this process will continue. Where the roof offers protection, the transformation will take somewhat longer.

This subtle metamorphosis points to the vitality of wood. I will explore this living material in the following lines,

Fig. 1

Fig. 2

Fig. 1
Shingle decoration to the eaves of a vernacular farm building.

Fig. 2
Barn below the Klanghaus with uniformly gray weathered facades. The intricate detailing of the shingle and vertical board envelope is particularly apparent around its openings and at the transitions between different surfaces.

addressing philosophical aspects that follow the tenets of new materialism.[1] This movement focuses on the meaning of materials and material culture and has become so significant that scholars in the arts and the humanities speak of a *material turn*. In this context, matter is seen not as a silent and passive resource but, rather, as an influential actor. This new materialism also questions both the division between nature and culture and the notion of human exceptionalism. In a building like the Klanghaus, such ideas are particularly important. Originally conceived by Marcel Meili and Andres Bosshard as an oversized sound installation, the architecture's further development by Staufer & Hasler also stems from its osmotic dialogue with its surroundings. This dialogue focuses less on the form than on the idea of the direct physical experience of the space. Sound waves can also be read as material, and they certainly interact physically with the material wood, which is caused to vibrate by the music.[2] As a result, material, people, space, and nature become equal participants in an event.

Wood is an archaic material: trees have existed for around 270 million years, which, in evolutionary terms, is a considerable length of time. And the specific wood with which we are concerned in this concrete case, spruce, even belongs to the one of the older orders of trees, the conifers. These have a somewhat simpler anatomic structure than deciduous trees. And yet their tissue is extremely diverse and plays a range of different roles. Wood principally consists of cellulose and lignin (from *lignum*, the Latin word for wood), and it is the latter that differentiates wood from a normal plant cell. The proportion of lignin is higher in conifers. The "actual" wood is formed from cambium. This layer is located between the phloem and the xylem—the two principal tissues—and is responsible for the secondary growth. It is the material secreted internally by cambium that we call wood or secondary xylem; the tissue secreted externally is known as bast or secondary phloem. If we saw

1 The term "new materialism" emerged at the end of the 1990s. The most important representatives and pioneers of the movement include Donna Haraway, Rosi Braidotti, Karen Barad, and Jane Bennett. One book that can be mentioned in this context is *Vibrant Matter* by Jane Bennett, Durham, N.C., 2010.

2 "The wood makes the architecture resound, in the aural and the visual, but also the haptic sense." From "Beinahe ein Instrument, Astrid Staufer, Andres Bosshard, Matthias Ruf im Dialog mit Marcel Meilis Thesen zum Klanghaus Toggenburg," in Carla Ferrer, Thomas Hildebrand and Celina Martinez-Cañavate (eds.), *Touch Wood, Material Architektur Zukunft*, Zurich, 2022, p. 189. The book appeared on the occasion of the exhibition *Touch Wood* in ZAZ BELLERIVE from June 10, 2022 to October 30, 2022.

Fig. 3

Fig. 4

Fig. 3
The shingle layer Martin Forrer installing mechanically split round shingles on the canopy soffit.

Fig. 4
Ruedi Vetsch splitting the 30-cm-long spruce shingles for the facade cladding.

a tree trunk in half, we see the growth rings or the cambium rings, which are created by the periodic activity of the cambium—at least at latitudes in which the climate is not constant. All this information[3] may sound abstract, but it is important to the shingle maker.

Handcraft based on ancient know-how

Not every part of a piece of wood is suitable for making shingles.[4] Put simply, the useful part is the central section between the sapwood (the outer, dynamically growing tissue of the trunk) and the innermost part, where the growth rings are too large. No longer physiologically active, the heartwood is dead. Unlike animals, plants have cell walls; these provide stability as the plant grows. This explains why trees can grow to heights of over one hundred meters. And it is important for the shingles, because the way a tree has grown influences the ability to split the wood. For the shingle maker, the choice of the right wood begins in the forest. There are trees that are ideal for producing shingles due to their growth and their condition. Only trees that meet specific criteria are suitable for being processed into shingles.[5] Traditionally, wood was—and still is—processed locally. In the case of Toggenburg, this wood is spruce. And since more compact wood is easier to split, only spruces with close and regular growth rings come into question. All these observations and this know-how, which has been passed down over centuries,[6] flow into these first of many steps in the process. One could say that the shingle-maker develops a relationship with the tree: with the living and the dead ones—those that have been felled. This leads to an interaction between humans and material that goes well beyond the mere exploitation of a resource. At the same time, it also suggests that the separation between humans and nature or between substance and form has become meaningless. And if we examine the processing of the shingle in more detail, this conclusion grows stronger.

3 In researching these questions I was able to count upon the support of my son, who was preparing for his biology exam at the ETH Zurich at the same time as I was writing this article. I generally understand knowledge as situated knowledge, in the sense set out by the philosopher Donna Haraway.

4 See the entry for shingle-making in the list of Switzerland's living traditions: https://www.lebendige-traditionen.ch/tradition/de/home/traditionen/die-schindelmacherei.html (last accessed on August 21, 2024).

5 Those interested in wood and shingles can find lots of information in this film: https://www.ardmediathek.de/video/handwerkskunst/wie-man-schindeln-herstellt/swr/Y3JpZDovL3N3ci5kZS9hZXgvbzE4MjM3MzU (last accessed on August 21, 2024).

6 Shingle-making is on the list of the living traditions in the Canton of Freiburg. See https://www.lebendige-traditionen.ch/tradition/de/home/traditionen-kantone/Freiburg.html (last accessed on August 21, 2024).

Fig. 5

Fig. 6

Fig. 5
Not a sliver is wasted, the wood determines the trajectory of the knife.

Fig. 6
The shingles are arranged in neat rows in boxes and stored in the nearby shed, ready to be laid.

After the tree has been felled in winter and the trunk, the so-called "Trämel," has been stored, the pieces cut in situ are marked on the side closest to the roots. This is because shingles are always laid in the direction of growth of the plant; the roots are placed below and the crown above. This ensures that water runs off them better.[7] The actual splitting of the shingles using the splitting blade demands practice and artisanal skill, especially when done by hand. The advantage of this approach is that it reduces damage to the fibers and, hence, ensures the impermeability of the shingles.

Half of the shingles used at the Klanghaus were split by the retired carpenter Ruedi Vetsch. He stood at the vice for up to four hours at a time, producing around 300 shingles a day.[8] Approximately 110,000 were made in total. The precisely dimensioned shingles were produced very close to the site, because his workshop is less than five minutes away—making this almost a "zero kilometer product." There is another interesting detail from the philosophical perspective, because the craft of splitting shingles is also an example of a notable phenomenon that the French philosophers Gilles Deleuze and Félix Guattari call "matter-movement," "matter-energy," or "matter-flow."[9] In their book *A Thousand Plateaus*, they criticize—and this criticism was also taken up by the thinkers of new materialism—the Aristotelian matter-form model, also known as the hylomorphic model, which requires a *previously* defined form and a homogeneous, passive material. We must, they say "add an energetic materiality in movement" to the matter. As an example, the two philosophers use the splitting of wood: "At any rate, it is a question of surrendering to the wood, then following where it leads by connecting operations to a materiality, instead of imposing a form upon a matter."[10]

7 See footnote 5.

8 See the account by Bettina Mittelstrass, "Jede von Hand," in *Klangmagazin*, January 2024.

9 Gilles Deleuze and Félix Guattari, *A Thousand Plateaus: Capitalism and Schizophrenia*, translated from the French by Brian Massimi, Minneapolis, 1987.

10 Ibid., p. 408.

Fig. 7

Fig. 8

Fig. 7
Typical scorched black triangles on spruce shingles, laid in a *Schlaufschirm* pattern where they overlap both vertically and laterally, after years of exposure to weather and sunlight on the south-facing side.

Fig 8
Testing of various shingle details in a 1:1 mock-up: The transition between a *Schlaufschirm* facade and a soffit of round shingles, along with a final row of shingles and an ornamental edge to the eaves. To the right, variants of the sharply pointed corner of the facade are visible.

Material and Philosophical Assemblage

According to this, the form of the shingles not only follows a specific tradition or an architectural idea, but is also the result of an intrinsic logic within the material, which is related to the process of growth. The anthropologist Tim Ingold identifies this as follows in his essay "An Ecology of Materials":[11] "The line that they [the axe or wedge] follow, is one that already grew in the wood when it was still part of the living tree and, hence, was part of its process of growth. Thus, the material, with which we work, is neither formless nor homogenous. It already *has* lines of growth, it has a grain, and the maker is not someone who forces a form upon the materials but, rather, someone who finds the grain and then adapts this to an emerging purpose."[12] The focus of these considerations is not what a material is, but what it does.

Hence, when a craftsman like Vetsch falls back on his experience, he is falling back on his knowledge of the *behavior* of the material. In this sense, wood is far from being a simple material or an object; rather, it harbors the potential for its own transformation. It is as if the process that occurs in the cells at a tiny scale is repeated during this processing. One could go further and say that, when a material "becomes architecture," this process represents the broadening of the relationship between two different entities. The same is suggested, for example, by the Italian philosopher Emanuele Coccia in his book *Metamorphoses*: "Since the world is the same for everyone and for all species, every act of design is also an act that blurs boundaries and disturbs the world of other species. Every time a bee, an oak tree, or a bacterium changes its environment to make its own life possible, this species also changes the environment of others. So architecture is not only the active relationship between a species and the world, but the necessary relationship between them.

11 Tim Ingold, "Eine Ökologie der Materialien," in Kerstin Stakemeier and Susanne Witzgall (eds.), *Macht des Materials—Politik der Materialität*, Zurich and Berlin, 2014. In this text, the author explicitly refers to the passage from Deuleuze/Guattari quoted above (footnote 10), trans. by R.H.

12 Ibid., p. 69.

Each species relates to others as an architect of the world. Architecture is not just a human affair, a cultural fact. It is not even the relationship between a species and a space, a form of life and its world. It is the paradigm of the interspecies relationship."[13] Coccia expands the approaches formulated by Deleuze and Guattari by adding a dimension that also includes more-than-human beings.

With regards to the term "assemblage," as used by Deleuze and Guattari,[14] I would like to conclude by returning to an architectural detail of the Klanghaus that was mentioned at the beginning of this article: the special structure of the facade of spruce shingles. The craft of shingle-laying is based on the joining together of individual elements to create a cloak of shingles. The end product is a weather-tight skin that is also fascinating at the aesthetic and haptic levels. Upon touching the skin, one is instinctively tempted to play upon it, as if it were an instrument. And while this may not be the underlying idea, I am convinced that I am not the only person to follow this impulse. At the same time, I am struck by another feature of this beautiful wooden cloak: the way in which this structure has an irregular pattern that recalls waves. This illustrates another characteristic of the "assemblage": smaller elements group together to form larger complexes, in this case, wave patterns.[15] The process of taking wood, transforming it manually into shingles, and then combining these to create a shingle facade is a combination of various forms of "assemblages": the cellular character of the wood with the split shingles that are then laid, at a slight offset, by the shingle layer. This is an example of the potentiation of and the interaction between different matter-flows, which respond to each other. Or, to conclude with a simple sentence from Meili's propositions: "The music listens and answers."[16]

13 Emanuele Coccia, *Metamorphoses*, translated from the French by Robin Mackay, Cambridge, 2021, p. 168.

14 Deleuze and Guattari 1987, p. 406. This term is also used in other texts by the duo.

15 See Ingold 2014: "One could draw the flow of the material as one wavy line and the flow of consciousness as another, and these two lines run more or less parallel with each other. Correspondence is about bringing these two lines in harmony with each other. Endeavoring to use an analogy from music, it is like when two melodies react contrapuntally to one another," trans. by R.H.

16 Marcel Meili, *Thesis Competition*, proposition 5, p. 29, here p. 22.

Klang·haus

Viviane Sonderegger

Klang·haus (*klˈaŋhaʊ͡s*), Nom. instr.
als (W)Ort vielsaitig,
benötigt lyrische Deklaration,
weil wenn 'ne Konstruktion
auf O-Ton trifft,
versetzt Poesie Schrift
sprachlich in Vibration;

→ absorbierend durchlesen

I. 1. "begeh(r)bares Resonanzwesen,"
auf kons(on) (t)anter Suche nach Anklang,
Kont·Akt der Inspiration;
→ Realisation einer alpinen Vision,
erfü(h)(l)lte Zukunft mit neuem Gesang;

Singt neutral, klingt vokal,
[*string.*] in Kata-Strophen;
ausgelöst durch schwingenden Akkord
(*senza. sord.*);

Zwar kein Alien,
aber ein Exot unter Klang-Arien,
→ [anat.] Torso *arioso* beginnt,
denkt [übers.] auch exper-i-(nstru)-mental;
spiegelt, wer wir wirklich sind
(ursp.) emotional;

Auffindbar bei Verbünde(l)ten im Feld
u. a. durch (Ein-)Klang auf dieser Welt;
macht uns ebf. zu (G)Ästen,

bis zu uns'ren roots vernetzt (i. weit. S. "verzweigt"),
weil Resonanz indiv. Ähnlichkeit aufzeigt;

Etwas, das vereint, nicht trennt:
sich selbst erfahr'n im Mo(nu)ment;
ein harmonisches Fundament
auf einer Grube (korr. "Talboden-Stube"),
[erw.] durch organische Reflektoren;

(lat.) "Äquivalent,"
menschlich, mechanisch, identisch
zu 'nem Trommelfell,
= Akustik zeigt sich visuell,
in Reiz-, Sinn-, Liebe-, voller Dynamik;

[ugs.] "Objekt mit Her(t)zschlag,"
mit Ochsenblut verziert,
Licht, Stimmung variiert
bei einatmender Reminiszenz
in seiner ursprünglichen Existenz;

Verlässt sich bei Intonation auf Intuition,
Bauchgefühl widerspiegelt verflossene Kadenz,
von Kopf bis (s. unten) Fuss[1],
zit. n. derselben Frequenz (engl. "*quote*");

Spekt(akulä)raler Anziehungspunkt,
strebt nach jmdm. der's versteht,
wenn's den Bogen* auch mal überspannt
unter'm *St(r)ich-Wort "*Magnet*";

Es existiert, weil's vibriert,
und wenn's resoniert, zieht sich's an
Land, nach neuen (U)fern oder nah suchend,
öhrenöffn-end-los, verlaufend,
sich reflektierend-(schw)irrend;
trifft den Nerv unserer Verbundenheit,
[*da capo*] von Raum & Zeit;

ebf. gezeichnet von Ornamenten,
besteht aus vielen verschiedenen Fragmenten,
aus sich berührenden Muster(n),
nahe beieinander liegend, wie ein Cluster;

1 -note.

[Org.] "Phänomen für Wider-(Sc)hall,"
frisch geschindelter (Kri)Stall,
(multi-)sinnlich gewordenes Intervall;
Begegnung zweier (Virtuo)Sinne(n),
wenn's wie wyld von Aussen nach Innen
funk(el)t;

Ein einheimisches Juwel,
(mit) Leib und Seel
[*colla parte*] (be-)spielbar,
bereits Realität gewordene Welle;
(ent-)führt den Menschen zurück zur Quelle,
dort schimmert jede Zelle als Accessoire;

Eine Erscheinung, die in uns was ruft:
z. B. Erinnerungen wach(-sen),
oder Einfluss hervor zu nehmen,
schafft neuen Campus
und das Vertrauen,
dass alles so (zurück-)kommt, wie's muss,
auch das, was wir in den Wald hinein;
es bestätigt, wir sind nicht allein:
auf Resonanzen können wir bauen.

bedeutet jmdm. (ggf. wieder) nähertreten,
(spezif.) beim Tanzen,
nicht auf der Nase herum,
sondern parabol im *crescendo*
sich verstärkend in (*Vol.*):

[arch.] “orchestriertes Medium,”
räsoniert über Beziehungen,
allein oder vor Publikum;
strebend nach *[hˈɑːmə͡ʊ]* nie
nach ’nem Echo der Apathie;
Frei in einer Feedback-Schlauf’,
etwas hört an, was anderes fängt auf/
bildet den Auftakt einer Symphonie;

(Allg.) gemeinsam durch Wände geh’n,
wieder aufzusteh’n,
wenn ein Ton (ge-)fällt;
wie erblühte Hackbrettrosetten,
durchlöchert in allen Facetten;

d. h. sich jemandem hingeben,
aufeinander eingehen/aneinander aufgehen,
erstrahlen wie z. B. Protz-E-Dur,
(Sig)Natur liegt selbst in der konkaven Figur,
siehe Abb.(-reviatur);

Impliziert komprimiert,
dass auch mal Stille (*pp*) genügt,
wenn wir unser Vergnügen stillen;
mal leise, mal laut Gesetz *(ff)*
erscheint, wenn etw./jmd. Interesse weckt,
oder uns was identisch ansteckt,
s. (engl. *“butterfly effect”*);

Ätherisches verfliegt potentiell,
deshalb ist die Frage essentiell:
Was ist schon von Dauer ohne Schönheit?
danach richtet sich die neue Baseline
durch Mark und Bein,
dürfen mehrere (T)Räume auf einmal sein.

Hearing with the Eyes. The Klanghaus as an "Experiment"

Astrid Staufer

What is this building, standing here in front of us in the landscape? Contemplating the completed work, I find myself looking both backward and forward in a conceptual exchange with my late colleague and friend Marcel Meili, and with Christian Zehnder, our current musical partner. Meili began the architectural narrative of the Klanghaus following the initiative of Peter Roth and created its theses before placing them into my hands.[1] Zehnder, after seven years as Artistic Director, is passing on this "walkable instrument" to the future with an impressive inaugural program.[2]

I An architectural experiment

So, what is actually standing here in front of us? Is it a pavilion? The Austrian baroque architect Fischer von Erlach demonstrated how to set buildings in the landscape. His imperial pleasure pavilion was a typology consisting of a center and wings that stretch into the landscape. Back then, emperors and archbishops commissioned constructions in this tri-part form: "models of ideal spaces," as Martin Feiersinger calls them.[3] But, he asks, what architectural typology is a pavilion, exactly? "A garden pavilion ... a walkable sculpture?"

Astoundingly, it is local democracy here in Toggenburg that has realized such a building, despite the *Neue Zürcher Zeitung's* claim of only a few years ago that "Eastern Switzerland does not exist," its politics, marked by numbing, fear- and envy-driven federalism, no longer spurring "any great ideas."[4] Now it has the Klanghaus. And a significant new idea.

Already, Toggenburg has produced two great bearers of new ideas: writer Ulrich Bräker and theologian Huldrych Zwingli. Now Toggenburg will be "the origin of an idea that radiates far and wide." In his theses, Meili describes the Klanghaus as "a point on the map that aspires to transform

1 Marcel Meili, "Neun Thesen und eine persönliche Nachbemerkung zum Entwurf für das Klanghaus Toggenburg," in Hochbauamt des Kantons St.Gallen, Amt für Kultur, Kanton St.Gallen, *Klanghaus Toggenburg,Thesenkonkurrenz/Thesis Competition. Bericht des Preisgerichts/ Report of the Jury*, 2010.

2 Christian Zehnder is a musician, singer, and composer. He was Artistic Director of the Klangwelt Toggenburg during the period of the creation of the Klanghaus between 2018 and its opening in 2025.

3 Martin Feiersinger, "Pavillons—Casinos—Follies. Eine zeichnerische Annäherung," in Andreas Nierhaus and Peter Husty (eds.), *Johann Bernhard Fischer von Erlach*, Salzburg and Vienna, 2023, pp. 65–73.

4 Andri Rostetter in *Neue Zürcher Zeitung*, November 14, 2022, p. 17.

Fig. 1

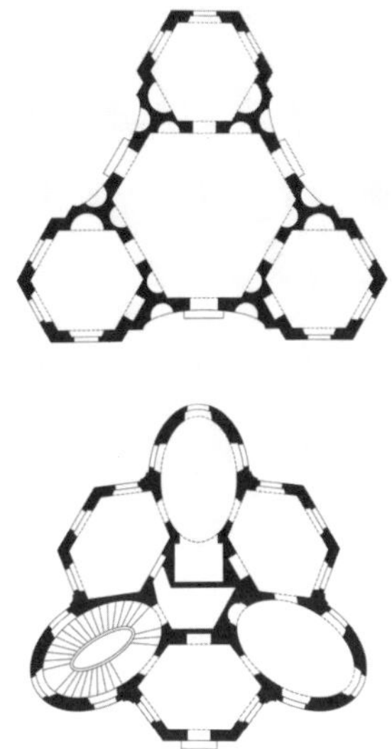

Fig. 2

Fig. 1
Model collage with and for Marcel Meili, 2019.

Fig. 2
Drawings by Martin Feiersinger at a scale of 1:100 of two garden buildings by Johann Bernhard Fischer von Erlach (1656–1723), presented under the title *Pavillons—Casinos—Follies. Eine zeichnerische Annäherung* in the exhibitions of Fischer von Erlach's work in Salzburg and Vienna, excerpt from the exhibition catalog 2023.

into a 'magic place'": a house as an "experiment." At the end of the day, the Klanghaus is just this, "the formal and physical embodiment of a musical experiment."[5] The term "experiment" describes a methodically designed investigation that seeks to empirically produce new insights. The focal point of this investigation is the process itself, as defined by the Latin verb *experiri*: to try, test, attempt, find out, experience.[6] Meili's is a broadly designed experiment for which he defined the criteria in his theses. This extraordinary starting point helped to ensure that the process has remained a research project until the very end, a fact that would have pleased him.

A first insight emerges from Meili's phrase "visual acoustics," suggesting a new relationship between building and sound. In purely acoustic terms, the range of viable potential forms for the various sound requirements is almost unlimited. But in the Klanghaus, the project permanently seeks motifs that use the eyes to open the ears and thus stimulate hearing through seeing. For example, the undulating irregularity of the shingles around the outdoor stages may disperse the sound waves en route to our ears; at the same time, however, these shingles guide our eyes so that our visual memory sensitizes our hearing. And the central space offers visual acoustics through the motif of oversized sound holes like those on hammered dulcimers.

The awareness of "the dominance of the sense of vision" in the age of digitalization, as described by Juhani Pallasmaa at the turn of the millennium in *The Eyes of the Skin*,[7] has generally encouraged the rediscovery of a lost multisensuality in architecture: not just the eye and the ear but the entire body, the hands, the feet, and the nose, should be involved in experiencing this "instrument." This occurs in individual moments, which begin when we take hold of the door handle of millennia-old bog wood, and continue as we move inside and grasp, literally and metaphorically, the turned balustrade to the staircase. Here, voices reverberate

5 Meili 2010, p. 21.

6 Cf. Lutz Mackensen, *Deutsche Etymologie. Ein Leitfaden durch die Geschichte des deutschen Wortes*, Berlin, Darmstadt, and Vienna, 1966, pp. 114 & 305.

7 Juhani Pallasmaa, *The Eyes of the Skin: Architecture and the Senses*, Chichester, 1996, p. 29.

Fig. 3

Fig. 3
Model collage with open "Isfahan doors" and an intercultural musical experiment (project version 2013).

in the resonance walls and feet thump on the cavity floor, while the aroma of alpine herbs or cowpats flows in through the ventilation flaps. With so much sensuality converging in one experience, there is a risk of teetering on the edge of architectural kitsch. This is avoided by embedding all these moments of perception into a larger whole: they are intertwined simultaneously in the space rather than being arranged sequentially. Each space has a powerful form, yet owes its complexity to this multisensuality and "multiple meaning"[8]—a term that was, incidentally, coined by Meili's friend and colleague Hermann Czech.

Multiple meaning is achieved in the Schafberg and Iltios music rooms by means of the glazed facade, which, curved for acoustic reasons, simultaneously intensifies the relationship with the landscape and lends a sculptural and spatial quality to the effect of contrast, which recalls the local art of paper-cutting.[9] In the Schafberg music room, this effect is vertically intensified: the lower, filter-like glazing anchors us in the space, while the mountain panorama opens up above. And in the Iltios music room, our eye can wander through the opening in the back wall and across the central space towards the Schwendisee, embedding the small (room) in the expansive (landscape). In the central space, a variety of spatial constellations can be created: the opening of a tall, narrow door towards the echo room transforms the spatial and acoustic effect; conversely, when the "Isfahan doors" are unfolded, the introverted experimental space converts into a concert hall overlooking the lake. These are constructed options that can be explored to make room for experimentation.

Given that trees grow skywards in more or less straight lines, a curvaceous timber building is also, naturally, a constructional experiment, one that Meili left us to carry out on the basis of his sketches. For the Klanghaus, these trees were bent, curved, and tapered so that they could form the "walkable instrument." Far removed from any traditional

8 Hermann Czech, the subject of a monograph by one of the coauthors of this publication, Eva Kuss, uses this term in, for example, his essay "Mehrschichtigkeit" (1977), in Hermann Czech, *Zur Abwechslung. Ausgewählte Schriften zur Architektur Wien*, Vienna, 1996, pp. 79–80.

9 Cf. the illustration "Scherenschnitt Toggenburg (Paper-cut from Toggenburg)" in Marcel Meili's theses on p. 26 of this publication, whose impact is also apparent in the series of photographs by Ladina Bischof.

Fig. 4

Fig. 5

Figs. 4–5
Even during the construction phase, lovers of experimentation were attracted to the Klanghaus like moths to a flame. Right: the Fürstenland Association of Alphorn Players on a spontaneous visit to the building site in summer 2024.

constructional logic, the task was to achieve numerous innovations in a transdisciplinary dialogue between planners, local artisans, and the cantonal construction authority, who consistently played an active and intelligent role in this "experiment."[10] Among these innovations are the vertical timber blocks, whose rounded connections resemble knee joints, the blunting of the sharp exterior edges of the shingle facade that separate one acoustic space from the next, or individual shingles that escape from a horizontal line as part of the "visual acoustics"—an innovation that initially, quite literally went against the grain for the artisans but ended up being a source of both pleasure and pride to them. Were it not for Meili's theses, who would ever have addressed such questions?

The cost pressures that grew over time eventually led to further, unforeseen experiments. For example, curved fiber-cement roof tiles now perform the unconventional function of cladding the base below the screen wall of manually split shingles. The role of snow guards on the roof is played by pan lids from a Swiss kitchenware manufacturer, which also provide a welcome at the entrance door. The unrelated—the traditional and the unusual—unite in symbioses: the volumetric "Isfahan walls" exemplify this. Thanks to Meili, they found their way from Persia to Toggenburg. Here, newly interpreted, they provide acoustic surprises. Their motifs are encountered again in the sound holes of hammered dulcimers, which trace their origins back to the same region and have been enriching the musical culture of Toggenburg since much earlier times. In the spirit of Meili, this exchange between tradition and innovation, between time-honored craft and the latest technology, between the familiar and the surprising, will also serve as a model for all that will happen in the Klanghaus in the future.

10 The cantonal construction authority demonstrated enormous respect for the "experiment" from the very beginning: following the accompaniment of the project by the Cantonal Building Director Werner Binotto from the competition to the execution project, the priorities were determined with the designer and user team in a first realization meeting chaired by Thomas Bürkle and Ralph Hagen. Of all the factors that had to be taken into account, the sentence "The Klanghaus is a walkable instrument" ended up playing a key role.

Fig. 6

Fig. 7

Fig. 6
Christian Zehnder in *Triohotala*, film still.

Fig. 7
Parabolically shaped external space with acoustic or hearing stage and "visual acoustics" in the shingle cladding. Over time, weathering below the overhanging coved eaves will inscribe the form of a second wave upon the undulating ornamentation behind the external stages. The exposed area of the screen wall of shingles will darken faster than the protected area.

II The musical experiment

Astrid Staufer in two conversations with Christian Zehnder, shortly before the completion of the Klanghaus in September 2024 and prior to its opening in April 2025

Christian Zehnder, we're reaching the end of the construction and of the book. What kind of building is this? Do we need such a house? And what and who convenes here?

The people of canton Appenzell live in a soft landscape, their natural yodelling is gentle, provoking the image of waves. In contrast, natural yodelling in Toggenburg has larger intervals, creating a larger, almost kicking movement. However, they don't sing in opposition to the mountains. They love their mountains, their animals, their elements: the wind, the weather, and everything else that comes with them. They honor the mountain, even if it harbors hardship and danger.

And the city folk? What will they bring?

A longing, triggered by overabundance and fragmentation, for simplicity and clarity. Such simplicity is found in the moving melodies sung by the farmers. Together, they create vibrations. The people of the city, on the other hand, have different acoustic ideas and a willingness to experiment that can foster dialogue. This requires openness. You need to want this, to be curious.

How can these be reconciled?

It's not about reconciliation; it's about the encounter and about mutual, shared interest. About growing together through dialogue. This exchange has always existed. Traditional music didn't emerge in the countryside alone: its adoption in towns and cities was a key factor in its development. But it's also about simultaneity. In cities there are "bubbles" that operate separately from each other. These usually don't overlap. Here, one group is the yodeling children's choir, a second is a symposium about urban noise, and a third is a drummer practicing in their room. In the Klanghaus, they simply can't ignore each other. This creates

Fig. 8

Fig. 9

Fig. 8
Entrance: welcomed by the ringing on pan lids.

Fig. 9
Zenithal light with the three "celestial ears," the obliquely angled conic skylights above the central space.

elementary opportunities for opening one's sensors, for inspiration and friction, and for mutual recharging. And this is precisely the experiment: we all long for harmony, but harmony can only be experienced if you also accept dissonance as part of the whole. The artistic curation of this process will continue to be extremely important in the future.

What does the Klanghaus give you as a musician?
The architecture enables me to be welcomed and supported as a listener. Everything makes sense and has its own intuitive logic. As I walk around the building, I can discover acoustic phenomena. People refer to "concert stages," but I prefer to call them "hearing stages." When you stand there and listen, you're at the center, like in a satellite dish. All the energy, every sound is focused on you and opens up the space for you in a new cosmos. However, you still remain part of the Earth; you remain rooted, standing at the heart of infinity.

And what happens to you inside the building?
The building isn't large, but it gives you a sense of security within this open landscape. It keeps you grounded. You feel supported and understood. As a musician, you always enter something ready to receive, so that inspiration can emerge from within. Inside the building, I become the accumulator in a power plant. I charge myself. The building recharges me and I begin to reverberate. It is I, not the building, who becomes the element of reverberation. The building is just a resonator. This is the key factor that distinguishes it: the fact that the room begins to reverberate with me. The normal concert hall reflects, but the Klanghaus resonates. The space "sings" along with its acoustic mirrors. They begin to reverberate and, in this moment, the building becomes an instrument. You don't experience anything like this anywhere else.

What do you as a musician think about the architectural space? What is its impact?

The central space is admittedly very intense, monumental and epic. One has to work with it, counter it in some way. This requires courage: I must bring the acoustic mirrors to life! If you attempt this experience, the space becomes active and gives a lot back. Then the space lifts you and your music to a new dimension. The cavities are reflectors, they make the sound more diffuse; there are convolutions that capture, shake up, and multiply the sound. This creates a sense of distance because sound waves in the space follow longer and more complex paths before reaching the ear. All of this offers you the opportunity to enter into the unexpected acoustic subtleties of a space and experience sound in a completely new way.

And the other music rooms?

The spatial highlight of the central space has a magnetic effect that enables one to fully concentrate and take something in very deeply. You can consolidate your experience here in the other, more pragmatic spaces. The possibilities are surprising: unity on the outside and what diversity within!

Given this diversity, why do we also need to be able to adjust the space by moving the doors—the "Isfahan double doors" and the door to the echo room?

This enables me to confront my music in different ways. On the one hand, I can reconfigure the spatial volumes and, on the other hand, I can experience acoustic changes by moving and altering my position in the space: piano—forte, adagio, allegro, presto. With what level of energy do I address the space? Every corner sounds different. My impression of the space is constantly, tangibly changing because it's built in such an exemplarily "open" way. This quality entices you to seek out the acoustic and musical experiment.

What is this musical experiment?

The Klanghaus is a place of inspiration and creation. It's a place where I can try out and experience my music in new ways; where I can spatially experiment with my ideas. But when we talk about "experimentation" in this context, this is also a major programmatic challenge for the Klangwelt, which will continue to require courage and precision. It won't be enough to regularly invite a few choirs and traditional musicians. The building challenges us to cross boundaries, to take risks. That's the experiment!
Let's stand in the Klanghaus and together look out towards the lake, towards the landscape, a vibrant ecosystem. The Klanghaus is also an ecosystem,

within and outside—a resonant biotope for all: dragonflies, worms, music lovers, nerds, sound researchers, traditional musicians, sound artists—for all that creeps, crawls, twitters, sings, and croaks. A biodiverse, sonorous nature reserve, with enough variety to ensure that something can occur that goes beyond what we already know. The Klanghaus isn't designed exclusively for traditional musicians or exclusively for new elites. It calls for diversity and new constellations that generate an open spirit and foster evolution.

Christian, let me conclude by repeating my question: What is this building that is standing here in front of you?

A building for listening and being astonished. A volume that I can cause to reverberate from the inside. A workshop, an open acoustic space in which to work where I find tools that enable me to try out and create new things. An acoustic body with a range of chambers for people who are addressing different things and questions simultaneously but who also want to cause each other to reverberate. A cosmopolitan acoustic body. The space becomes a tool that allows us to immerse ourselves in new "acoustic perspectives" and ideas. A space for new acoustic experiences that go beyond the boundaries. I hope every musician who comes here can experience a pivotal moment in a new direction. The building should remain an experiment in the future: a resonant microcosm, varied, surprising, open. Toggenburg needs diversity.

Isn't this a threat to the authenticity of the local musical culture?

Our bases are the identities that have developed over generations. We begin with the acoustic cosmos of Toggenburg, its culture, its sounds; these are the foundations of our building. This is our inventory; it should all remain present and tangible at all times. It's our responsibility to ensure that this culture can keep flourishing here and continue to evolve, and that it's capable of and willing to have a place here going forward. We provide the spaces for this.

We open the doors!

Responsible Project Participants from the Initial Idea to the Realization of the Klanghaus

Fig. 1 Topping-out ceremony, August 17, 2023.

Roth, Peter, Initiator of the Klangwelt and the Klanghaus, Musician, Conductor, Composer

Canton of St.Gallen
- Bucher, Laura, Cantonal Councilor, Head of the Department of Home Affairs
- Damann, Bruno, Cantonal Councilor, Head of the Health Department (former Head of the Department of Economic Affairs)
- Gut, Daniel, Cantonal Councilor, President of the Advisory Committee, Resolution of the Cantonal Government regarding the construction of the Klanghaus Toggenburg (2015/16, 2018/19)
- Haag, Willi, former Cantonal Councilor, Head of the Construction and Environment Department
- Hartmann, Susanne, President of the Cantonal Government, Head of the Construction and Environment Department
- Hilber, Kathrin, former Cantonal Councilor, Cantonal Councilor of Home Affairs
- Klöti, Martin, former Cantonal Councilor, Head of the Department of Home Affairs
- Mächler, Marc, Cantonal Councilor, Head of the Finance Department (former Head of the Construction and Environment Department)
- Tinner, Beat, Cantonal Councilor, Head of the Department of Economic Affairs

Region of Toggenburg
- Bürge, Pius, former Cantonal Councilor, IG Klanghaus
- Friedli, Esther, Member of the Council of States, First Signatory of the petition and participant in the Expert Workshop
- Gunzenreiner, Alois, Mayor of Wattwil
- Looser, Kilian, former Cantonal Councilor, Mayor of Nesslau
- Sailer, Martin, Cantonal Councilor, Board Member of Südkultur
- Spoerlé, Christian, Cantonal Councilor, former President of Kultur Toggenburg
- Thalmann, Linus, former Cantonal Councilor
- Widmer, Andreas, former Cantonal Councilor

Municipality of Wildhaus-Alt St. Johann
- Diezig, Thomas, Mayor
- Ebneter, Alois, former Mayor
- Municipal Council
- Syz, Rolf, former Mayor of Wildhaus
- Züllig, Rolf, former Mayor

Construction Authority, Canton of St.Gallen
- Binotto, Werner, former Cantonal Building Director
- Bürkle, Thomas, Project Developer
- Doguoglu, Erol, Cantonal Building Director
- Fankhänel, Jens, former Project Developer
- Fischer, Michael, former Cantonal Building Director
- Hagen, Ralph, Project Manager
- Luzio, Adelbert, former Project Manager
- Strehlau, Jürgen, former Project Developer
- Vaucher, Sacha, Project Manager
- Zünd, Bruno, former Project Manager

Cultural Office, Canton of St.Gallen
- Brunnschweiler, Sabina, Co-Head of Office
- Eicher, Florian, former Deputy Head of Office
- Hartmann, Edi, former Project Manager
- Meier, Katrin, former Head of Office
- Rühle, Christopher, Co-Head of Office
- Scartazzini, Tanja, former Head of Office
- Schmid, Hans, former Head of Office
- Schwarz, Andreas, Head of Strategic Projects and Deputy Head of Office

Klangwelt Toggenburg Foundation, Foundation Board
- Bütikofer, Hans, former President of the Foundation
- Diezig, Thomas
- Ebneter, Alois, former member
- Eppenberger, Matthias, former member
- Grob, Jacques, former President of the Foundation
- Hegi, Fritz, former member
- Hilber, Kathrin, former President of the Foundation
- Kamm, Barbara
- Klöti, Martin, former member
- Lorétan, Guy
- Maiss, Sebastian, former member
- Manser, Gabriela, former member
- Meier, Katrin, former member
- Müller, Mathias, President of the Foundation
- Ostendarp, Hermann
- Roth, Peter, former member
- Roth, Ueli, former member
- Schlumpf, Martina
- Schmid, Christian, former member
- Schwarz, Andreas
- Vincenz, Reto, former member
- Züllig, Rolf, former member

Klangwelt Employees
- Gygax, Raphael, former CEO
- Hadorn, Mirjam, CEO
- Haller, Stephan K. former CEO
- Hartmann, Edi, Head of Operations
- Müller, Andreas B., former CEO
- Räss, Nadja, Yodeler, former Intendant
- Rohner-Grob, Christina, former CEO
- Zehnder, Christian, Artistic Director

Further Project Participants
- 1,400 members of the IG KLANGHAUS TOGGENBURG
- 10,000 signatories of the petition
- Ammann, Matthias, Organizer of the flash mob
- Baumann, Raphael, Klangcampus project group
- Blatter, Daniel, Region Toggenburg, Klanghaus 2.0 taskforce
- Büsser, Flavio, pre-project steering committee
- Dörler, Anita, pre-project steering committee
- Gämperle, Christof, pre-project steering committee
- Höhener, Hans, pre-project steering committee
- Humbel, Daniel, Klangcampus project group
- Kuratli, Peter, pre-project steering committee
- Nadig, Max, Toggenburg Tourist Board, Klanghaus 2.0 taskforce and Klangcampus project group
- Riederer, Ferdinand, pre-project steering committee
- Schmid, Hubertus, pre-project steering committee
- Stump, Roland, Hotelier, Stump's Alpenrose, Klangcampus project group
- The Board and 1,000 members of the Committee of Friends of the Klangwelt

Foundations supporting the Klanghaus and Klangcampus
- Annette Ringier-Stiftung
- Ernst Göhner Stiftung
- Hamasil Stiftung
- Jubiläumsstiftung der Schweizerischen Mobiliar
- Lienhard Stiftung
- Looser, Alex
- Looser, Hugo
- Looser, Leo and Marcella
- Otto und Veronika Kägi Stiftung
- Räbsamen, Urs

- Schiess, Fritz and Marie-Claude
- Steinegg Stiftung
- Stiftung Temperatio
- Stocker-Looser, Irma
- Susanne und Martin Knechtli-Kradolfer Stiftung
- U.W. Linsi-Stiftung

ARCHITECTURE AND CONSTRUCTION MANAGEMENT

Meili, Peter, Architekten
- Meili, Marcel, Architect and Author of the Entry to the Thesis Competition with Kevin Demierre

Staufer & Hasler Architekten
- Holenstein, Moritz, Architect and former Project Manager, Klanghaus construction project
- Ruf, Matthias, Architect and Project Manager, Klanghaus execution design and realization
- Staufer, Astrid, Architect with responsibility for the Klanghaus Project
- Uhl, Annette, Architect with responsibility for the execution design of the building services
- Woerz, Marcel, Architect and Construction Manager, Klanghaus construction project

- Bretscher, Walter, Construction Manager, cost estimate

Bauseits Partner
- Hess, Simone, Construction Manager
- Höpli, Matthias, Construction Manager
- Müller, Thomas, Overall Project Manager

SPECIALIST DESIGNERS AND DISCIPLINES

Applied Acoustics
- Kessler, Dominik, Acoustician
- Lachmann, Martin, Acoustician

Bivgrafik
- Irion, Kristin, Signage Consultant

Bosshard, Andres, Sound Artist

Conzett, Bronzini Partner
- Conzett, Jürg, Civil Engineer, bridge
- Verginer, Roman, Civil Engineer, bridge
- Création Holz
- Blumer, Hermann, Timber Building Engineer

Création Holz
- Blumer, Hermann, Holz-bauingenieur

EBP Schweiz
- Jud, Ramon, Project Manager, electrical design
- Ott, Erich, Overall Project Manager, HVACSE
- Pazmiño Friesecke, Mirco, Project Manager, HVAC
- Richter, Heinz, Overall Project Manager, construction project
- Schürmann, Patrick, Project Manager, building automation
- Stagliano, Rosetta, Project Manager, sanitary design
- Wettstein, Rolf, former Project Manager electrical design

Fiorio Fassadentechnik
- Fiorio, Marco, Facade Designer

FKL & Partner
- Durot, Roger, Civil Engineer & Geometer

H PLUS S
- Hofer, Brigitt, Foodservice Designer
- Krebs, Pascal, Foodservice Designer

Lichtsektor
- Brenner, Matthias, Lighting Designer
- Hermann, Raphael, Lighting Designer

Mühlebach Partner
- Hofmann, Ursula, Building Physicist
- Mühlebach, Andreas, Building Physicist

Richard Widmer Analysen
- Berchtold, Bernhard, Sanitary Designer
- Schär, Hans, HVAC Engineer
- Widmer, Richard, HVAC Engineer, natural ventilation

SJB Kempter Fitze
- Bergamin, Corinne, Construction Engineer
- Fischinger, Dominik, Timber Building Engineer
- Gadient, Marcel, Fire Protection Planner
- Meier, Christoph, Overall Project Manager
- Rick, Stefan, Timber Building Engineer
- Schmon, Philipp, Construction Engineer
- Wick, Sandro, Construction Engineer

Tingo
- Baumann, Andreas, AV Planner
- Wenzel, Hansjörg, AV Planner

Vogt Landschaftsarchitekten
- Kroll, Simon, Landscape Architect
- Ruge, Lars, Landscape Architect
- Vogt, Günther, Landscape Architect

EXECUTION

Abderhalden Holzbau
- Abderhalden, Christoph, Sub-Project Manager

Alpstein Kälte
- Locher, Markus, Project Manager, cooling technology

Amendola
- Panic, Marko, Project Manager, underfloor heating

Andreas Bischof
- Bischof, Andreas, CEO, Project Manager, joinery work
- Eberle, Rolf, Assembly Manager, joinery work

AS Aufzüge
- Bischof, Simon, Project Manager

AUVISO Audio Visual Solutions
- Lerch, Daniel, Project Manager, audio systems

Bichler + Partner
- Ibrovic, Haris, Assembly Manager, electrical work
- Stettler, Lukas, Project Manager, electrical work

Blumer–Lehmann
- Bischoff, Stephan, Project Manager, timber building
- Bollhalder, Raphael, Foreman
- Frick, Ursula, expanded geometry and parametric design
- Huber, Simon, Foreman
- Jung, Remo, Foreman
- Jussel, Richard, Overall Project Manager
- Studerus, Michael, Project Manager, AVOR

Bodarto
- Küpfer, Roman, Project Manager, tiling

Brändle Bedachungen
- Ammann, Josias, CEO
- Clajus, Marco, Metal Roofer
- Forrer, Martin, Shingle Layer

E. Weber
- Frischknecht, Roger, Project Manager, roadbuilding

Geisser Innenausstattung
- Geisser, Ruedi, CEO, Project Manager
- Rust, Andreas, Assembly Manager

Huka-Baupool
- Bollhalder, Daniel, Foreman
- Dürr, Martin, Project Manager, construction

Koster Holzwelten
- Laager, Marco, Assembly Manager, doors
- Urscheler, Mathias, Project Manager, doors

Kuhn Rikon
- Gerfin, Tobias, CEO, Supplier, pan lids

Kunstgiesserei St.Gallen
- Badertscher, Gabriel, Project Manager, signage elements

Lippuner Energie- und Metallbautechnik
- Gantenbein, Marc, Project Manager
- Schwendener, Rudolf, Assembly Manager

Malerbetrieb Grob
- Grob, Andreas, Project Manager

Markus Baumann
- Baumann, Markus, Project Manager, paneling

Metallatelier
- Fuchs, David, Project Manager, acoustic mirrors & echo cushions
- Riegger, Sunyam Emanuel, Assembly Manager, acoustic mirrors & reverb cushions

Metallraum
- Keller, Randy, Assembly Manager, metalwork
- Schnetzer, Hansjürg, Project Manager, metalwork

Pius Nadler
- Scheidegger, Michel, Project Manager, foodservice construction
- Schenkel, Roland, Project Manager, foodservice construction

Pozzi
- Oberholzer, Benjamin, Project Manager, bridge construction

Riget
- Pfiffner, Roman, Project Manager, scaffolding

Ruedi Vetsch, Shingle Maker

S. Brunner Malerei
- Brunner, Sereina, Painter

Schreinerei Stolz
- Abderhalden, Silvia, Project Manager
- Feurer, Lukas, Project Manager
- Frick, Marco, Assembly Manager
- Stolz, Christoph, CEO

Schöb
- Bühler, Philipp, Project Manager, joinery work
- Koller, Thomas, CEO

Simconex
- Böhler, Réne, Project Manager, building automation
- Pertler, Stefan, Project Manager, building automation

Tobler Lüftung & Klima
- Forchini, Giovanni, Project Manager
- Schoch, Adrian, Project Manager

Tomwerk
- Giger, Tom, responsibility for doors, attenuation, acoustic mirrors

Urs Oberholzer Sanitär
- Oberholzer, Urs, Project Manager

Wilhelm Büchel
- Lampert, Marc, Project Manager, garden construction

Biographies

Ladina Bischof has been working as a freelance photographer since 2013 and has been represented by Agentur 13 Photo since 2022. She portrays people and their surroundings by taking a documentary approach. Her interest in simplicity leads her to avoid dramatic staging. She lives and works in St.Gallen.

Erol Doguoglu studied architecture at ETH Zurich and heads the Building Authority of the Canton of St.Gallen in the role of Cantonal Building Director.

Mirjam Fischer studied art and architectural history and modern German literature in Bern. Through her company mille pages, she acts as an independent book producer and publisher in the area of art, photography, and design for a range of institutions and publishing houses. Prior to this, she was Head of Publications at the Museum für Gestaltung Zürich and Publishing Director at Edition Patrick Frey. Mirjam Fischer lives and works in Zurich.

Sabine von Fischer explores the interactions between architecture and acoustics, reviews programs for architecture and engineering competitions, and takes on science writing and essays. She is also a freelance artist and writer including publications *Das akustische Argument* (2019) and *Architektur kann mehr. Von Gemeinschaft fördern bis Klimawandel entschleunigen* (2023).

Christian Gressbach is a tourism expert. He studied tourism and sport management in Chur, Breda (NL), and Bayreuth (D). A native of Toggenburg, he is a professor at the University of Applied Sciences of the Grisons, where he is on the staff of the Institute for Tourism and Leisure. He is also the Managing Director of the Toggenburg Tourist Board. One of the main focuses of his research is resonance tourism.

Lea Hagmann was awarded a doctorate in ethnomusicology at the University of Bern, where she heads the Master's program in World Arts and Music. Alongside her academic activities, she also works in the music department of Radio SRF2 Kultur and released her first cinema film, *Beyond Tradition: Kraft der Naturstimmen*, in 2023 in cooperation with the film team of the Toggenburg production company ExtraMileFilms.

Susanna Koeberle is a freelance journalist, author, and curator. She studied German studies, comparative literature, philosophy, and art history in Zurich and Paris. She writes about art, design, and architecture in a range of Swiss media and regularly contributes to art publications. She has a special interest in the interfaces and the dialogue between different disciplines.

Eva Kuss studied architecture at Graz University of Technology, ETH Zurich, and the University of Applied Arts Vienna, where she received her doctorate in 2014. She has run the architectural office coabitare in Graz since 2009. Her book *Hermann Czech. An Architect in Vienna* was published by Park Books in 2018 (D) / 2023 (E). Hermann Czech and Marcel Meili were associated for many years as both colleagues and professional collaborators (as exemplified by the interiors for Swiss Re in Rüschlikon, which Czech developed together with Adolf Krischanitz).

Axel Langer is an art historian and has been working as a curator at the Museum Rietberg in Zurich for a quarter of a century. He is responsible for the art of Western Asia and is particularly interested in Persia's cultural interaction with Europe and India. His most recent exhibition was dedicated to the putative prohibition of images in Islam. He is also interested in typography and collects gramophone records.

Sonja Lieberherr-Schnyder grew up in Obertoggenburg. Having sung and yodeled in various groups since she was a child, she recites the Alpine blessing and is a custodian of Toggenburg's musical heritage. At the same time, she has a strong connection with the present day and with other cultures.

Marcel Meili studied architecture at ETH Zurich and founded the office Meili, Peter Architekten in Zurich with Markus Peter in 1987. He taught at the International Summer Academy in Berlin, Zurich University of the Arts, and Harvard University in Cambridge, USA. In 1999, he was appointed to a professorship at ETH Zurich, where he carried out research into the built future of Switzerland in Studio Basel alongside Jacques Herzog, Pierre de Meuron, Roger Diener, and Christian Schmid. In his roles as teacher and mentor, he and his methodical passion significantly influenced generations of Swiss architects. Marcel Meili died in 2019 after a long and serious illness.

Alfred Messerli is a titular professor of the University of Zurich and teaches and researches at ISEK—the Department of Social Anthropology and Cultural Studies, having also spent time in Bremen, Pavia, and Geneva between 2001 and 2019. He has worked on children's folklore and the spreading of literacy in Switzerland. Further focuses of his many publications include narratology, self-observation, research into the mass use of images, and the history of reading.

Norm. Dimitri Bruni and Manuel Krebs studied graphic design at the School of Design in Biel. In 1999, they co-founded the graphic design studio Norm. Ludovic Varone studied visual communication at Zurich University of the Arts ZHdK and joined the collective in 2005. The focus of Norm's work is book and font design.

Peter Roth, born in St.Gallen, is a musician, composer, choirmaster, and speaker. His musical work is closely connected with his adopted home of Toggenburg. He has directed the choir of the Evangelical Church of Alt St. Johann since 1973 and the Chorprojekt St.Gallen since 1989. The "Toggenburg Passion" and "Media vita," the requiem for Niklaus Meienberg, are outstanding examples of his empathy and musicality. In 2001, he initiated the Klangwelt Toggenburg, which now vibrantly shares the musical tradition of Toggenburg through courses, the Natural Voices Festival, the Klangschmiede, and the Klanghaus.

Matthias Ruf followed his apprenticeship as an architectural draftsman by studying architecture at ZHAW Winterthur and Berlin University of the Arts (UdK), where he spent a semester. Since 2012, he has worked as an architect at Staufer & Hasler Architekten, where he became an associate in 2024. Between 2019 and 2025 he was the Project Leader for the Klanghaus Toggenburg, acquiring broad expertise in the areas of timber building, acoustics, and sound. He is currently researching into and writing about the Appenzellerhaus and timber construction.

Viviane Sonderegger grew up in Speicher in Appenzell Ausserrhoden. She studied at the Institute of Musicology at the University of Bern. In 2022, she was awarded the "Young Talent" prize of the Literature Section of the International Lyceum Club St.Gallen. Viviane Sonderegger is currently living as a freelance poet and animal communicator in Welschenrohr/Solothurn.

Astrid Staufer studied at ETH Zurich (where her teachers included Marcel Meili) and has headed the architectural office Staufer & Hasler in Frauenfeld, Zurich, alongside Thomas Hasler since 1994. She was Head of the Institute for Constructive Design at ZHAW, a lecturer at ETH Zurich, and a professor at ETH Lausanne, and has been Professor of Building Construction and Design at Vienna University of Technology since 2011. She designed and realized the RiffRaff cinema and apartment project in Zurich in collaboration with Meili, Peter Architekten. From 2012, she developed the construction project for the Klanghaus together with Marcel Meili and her office. Following his death in 2019, she and her office worked to realize the project in his spirit.

Ueli Steingruber has been working as a freelance photographer in St.Gallen since 2015. After training as a print designer and working in an agency he studied photography at a vocational college. Permanently on the lookout for subtle and authentic moments, his current focus is reportage photography.

Andrea Wiegelmann publishes on issues of spatial planning and housing, as well as sustainable developments in urban planning and architecture. In 2015, she and Kerstin Forster founded Triest Verlag in Zurich. She was responsible for communication at the ArchitekturWerkstatt St.Gallen and held a teaching position at TU Kaiserslautern; since autumn 2024 she has been Deputy Director of Studies for the Bachelor's program in architecture at HTA Fribourg. She is a board member of the Architektur Forum Ostschweiz.

Christian Zehnder's musical training includes the study of both jazz music and classical singing (baritone). In 1996, he founded the duo Stimmhorn together with Balthasar Streiff. As a director and composer in musical theater he created extraordinary productions that shifted the boundaries between music, theater, performance, and sound art. His honors include the prestigious "Albert Mountain Award." He has been Artistic Director of the Klangwelt Toggenburg since 2019.

Literature

Sabine von Fischer, Approaching Sound

- Andres Bosshard, *Stadt hören: Klangspaziergänge durch Zürich*, Zurich, 2009.
- Sabine von Fischer, *Das akustische Argument. Wissenschaft und Hörerfahrung in der Architektur des 20. Jahrhunderts*, Zurich, 2019.
- Martin Lachmann, "Schall und Rauch," in *TEC21*, 11/2012, pp. 16–19.
- Martin Lachmann, "... Ohren, die nicht hören...," in *TEC21*, 11/2012, pp. 20–25.

Christian Gressbach, In Search of Resonance

- Herzog & de Meuron and Studio Noun, "Arealstudie Klangcampus. Räumliches Entwicklungskonzept und architektonisches Leitbild," Klangwelt Toggenburg Foundation, 2021/22.
- Verena Muntschick, Anja Kirig et al., *Der neue Resonanz-Tourismus*, Rottweil, 2019.
- Hartmut Rosa, *Resonanz: Eine Soziologie der Weltbeziehung*, Frankfurt a. M., 2016.

Lea Hagmann with Sonja Lieberherr-Schnyder, In Harmony with Nature

- Raymond Ammann, Andrea Kammermann, and Yannick Wey, *Jodeln im Kopf. Erkenntnisse einer musikkognitiven Untersuchung im Alpsteingebiet*, Zurich, 2021.
- Barney G. Glaser and Anselm L. Strauss, *Grounded Theory. Strategien qualitativer Forschung*, Bern, 2005.
- Juniper Hill and Caroline Bithell, "An Introduction to Music Revival as Concept, Cultural Process, and Medium of Change," in Caroline Bithell and Juniper Hill (eds.), *The Oxford Handbook of Music Revival*. Oxford and New York, 2014, pp. 3–42.
- Thomas Krefeld, "Die 'emische' und die 'etische' Forschungsperspektive," in *Lehre in den Digital Humanities*, 2020, see dh-lehre.gwi.uni-muenchen.de, (accessed on September 1, 2024).
- R. Murray Schafer, *The Soundscape. Our Sonic Environment and the Tuning of the World*, Rochester, Vermont, 1993 [1977].
- Christopher G. Small, *Musicking. The Meanings of Performing and Listening*, Middletown, Connecticut, 1998.
- Timothy Taylor, "Music on the move, as object, as commodity," in J. R. McNeill and Kenneth Pomeranz (eds.), *The Cambridge World History*, vol. VII, part II "Shared Transformations?," Cambridge, 2015, pp. 205–24.

Susanna Koeberle, The Material Vitality of Shingles

- Jane Bennett, *Lebhafte Materie*, Berlin, 2020.
- Rosi Braidotti, *Posthumanismus*, Frankfurt a. M., 2024.
- Emanuele Coccia, *Metamorphosen*, Munich, 2021.
- Gilles Deleuze and Félix Guattari, *A Thousand Plateaus: Capitalism and Schizophrenia*, translated from the French by Brian Massimi, Minneapolis, 1987.

- Tim Ingold, “Eine Ökologie der Materialien”, in Kerstin Stakemeier and Susanne Witzgall (eds.), *Macht des Materials—Politik der Materialität*, Zurich and Berlin, 2014.

Eva Kuss, A Built Resonator
- Eva Kuss, *Hermann Czech. An Architect in Vienna*, Zurich, 2023.

Axel Langer, Holes in the Wall
- Hassan Azad, “Ali Qapu: Persian Historical Music Room,” in *akuTEK, Proceedings of the Institute of Acoustics*, vol. 30, part 3, 2008 (https://www.akutek.info/Papers/HA_Persian.pdf).
- Sussan Babaie, *Isfahan and Its Palaces: Statecraft, Shi‘ism and the Architecture of Conviviality in Early Modern Iran*, Edinburgh, 2008.
- Mehreen Chida-Razvi, “From Function to Form: *Chini-khana* in Safavid and Mughal Architecture,” in *South Asian Studies*, vol. 35, no. 1, 2019, pp. 82–106.
- Eugenio Galdieri, *Esfahan: ‘Ali Qapu: An Architectural Survey*, Rome, 1979.
- Linda Komaroff, “Chinese Porcelains from the Ardabil Shrine: Collecting and Display in Iran,” in Ali M. Ansari and Melanie Gibson (eds.), *Fruit of Knowledge, Wheel of Learning: Essays in Honour of Carole and Robert Hillenbrand*, London, vol. 2, 2022, pp. 268–85.
- Thomas Ogger, “Hafiz und Goethe, ihre Sprache und Musik,” in *Spektrum Iran. Zeitschrift für islamisch-iranische Kultur*, 26th yr., no. 4, 2013, pp. 84–105.
- Esther Schmidt, “Negotiating Cosmopolitan Taste with Local Culture: Porcelain Rooms in Indian Forts and Palaces,” in Jon Stobart (ed.), *Global Goods and the Country House: Comparative Perspectives, 1650–1800*, London, 2023, pp. 307–330.

Marcel Meili, Thesis Competition
- Marcel Meili, “Neun Thesen und eine persönliche Nachbemerkung zum Entwurf für das Klanghaus Toggenburg,” in Hochbauamt des Kantons St.Gallen, Amt für Kultur, Kanton St.Gallen, *Klanghaus Toggenburg. Thesenkonkurrenz/Thesis Competition. Bericht des Preisgerichts/Report of the Jury*, 2010, pp. 20–35.
- Brigitte Bachmann-Geiser, *Das Alphorn in der Schweiz*, Bern, 1976.
- Brigitte Bachmann-Geiser, *Die Volksmusikinstrumente der Schweiz*, Leipzig, 1981.
- Willi and Ursula Dolder, *Rund um den Säntis*, Zurich, 1992.
- Diego Giovanoli, *Alpschermen und Maiensässe in Graubünden*, Bern, 2004.
- Edwin Huwyler, *Die Bauernhäuser der Kantone Obwalden und Nidwalden*, Basel, 1993.
- Angelus Hux and Alexander Troehler, *Klangräume. Kirchen und Orgeln im Thurgau*, Frauenfeld, 2007.
- Herbert Maeder, *Appenzell—Land und Leute*, Zurich, 1996.
- János Manga, *Ungarische Volkslieder und Volksinstrumente*, Corvina, 1969.
- Rolf Meier, *Das Bauernhaus im Toggenburg*, Bern, 1974.
- Christoph Mayr Fingerle, *Neues Bauen in den Alpen—Architekturpreis 1995*, Basel, 1996.
- Christoph Mayr Fingerle, *Neues Bauen in den Alpen—Architekturpreis 1999*, Basel, 2000.
- Christoph Mayr Fingerle, *Neues Bauen in den Alpen—Architekturpreis 2006*, Basel, 2007.
- Joachim Moroder and Benno Peter, *Hotelarchitektur—Bauten und Projekte für den Tourismus im alpinen Raum 1920–1940*, Innsbruck, 1993.
- Dieter Ringli, *Schweizer Volksmusik—Von den Anfängen um 1800 bis zur Gegenwart*, Altdorf, 2006.
- Andreas Schwab, *Monte Verità—Sanatorium der Sehnsucht*, Zurich, 2003.
- Andreas Schwab and Claudia Lafranchi, *Sinnsuche und Sonnenbad*, Zurich, 2001.
- *St. Moritz und das Engadin*, in *Merian*, no. 2, Feb. 1981.
- Harald Szeemann, *Monte Verità—Berg der Wahrheit*, Venice, 1978.
- Marc Treib, *Space Calculated in Seconds, The Philips Pavilion*, Princeton, 1996.

Films:
- Thomas Lüchinger, *Johle und Werche*, 2007 (also source of images).
- Cyrill Schläpfer, *Ur-Musig*, 2003.
- Stefan Schwietert, *Das Alphorn*, 2003 (also source of images).
- Stefan Schwietert, *Heimatklänge*, 2007 (also source of images).

Alfred Messerli, Songs from the Heart
- Ulrich Bräker, *The Life Story and Real Adventures of the Poor Man of Toggenburg*, transl. by Derek Bowman, Edinburgh, 1970.
- Ulrich Bräker, *Sämtliche Schriften in 5 Bänden. Bearbeitet von Andreas Bürgi, Alfred Messerli et al.*, 5 vols., vols. I–III, Munich, 1998, vol. IV, Munich, 2000, vol. V, Munich, 2010.
- Ebel, Joh.[ann] Gottfried, *Schilderung der Gebirgsvölker der Schweiz*, 2 vols., Leipzig, 1798, 1802.
- Johann Gottfried Herder (ed.), *Volkslieder*, 2 vols., Leipzig, 1778, 1779.
- Johann Rudolf Steinmüller, *Beschreibung der schweizerischen Alpen- und Landwirthschaft, nach den verschiedenen Abweichungen einzelner Kantone*, 2 vols., Winterthur, 1804.

Mathias Ruf, An Accessible Instrument
- Regine Abegg and Christine Barraud Wiener, *Kunstdenkmäler des Kanton Zürichs*, new edition, vol. II.I, Bern, 2002.
- Mihaly Bariska, “Physik der Seiteninstrumente: am Beispiel der Violine,” in *Schweizerische Zeitschrift für Forstwesen*, vol. 147, 1996.
- Rea Brändle, *Ammanns Vermächtnis, Aus dem Leben des Toggenburger Instrumentenmachers Ulrich Ammann*, Schwellbrunn, 2010.
- Ulrich Conrads and Bernhard Leitner, “Der Hörbare Raum. Erfahrungen und Mutmassungen,” in *Daidalos*, no. 17, 1985, pp. 28–46.
- Victoir Desarnaulds and Yves Loerincik, “Vases acoustiques dans les églises du Moyen Age,” in *Mittelalter, Moyen Age, Medioevo, Temp medieval: Zeitschrift des Schweizer Burgenvereins*, no. 6, 2001, pp. 65–72: fig.
- “Kantonsratsbeschluss über den Bau des Klanghauses Toggenburg,” https://www.ratsinfo.sg.ch/gremium/468/geschaefte/3635#documents.
- Athanasius Kircher, *Neue Hall- und Thon-Kunst, Oder Mechanische Gehaim-Verbindung der Kunst und Natur, durch Stimme und Hall-Wissenschafft gestifftet*, Ellwangen, 1684, https://digital.slub-dresden.de/werkansicht/dlf/1420/1.
- Aline Kottmann, *St. Walburga in Meschede. Der karolingische Bau und das Schalltopfensemble*, Büchenbach, 2015.
- Werner Lottenmoser, “Von der Akustik der Geige,” in *Physikalische Blätter*, 1978.
- Marcel Meili, “Gedanken zum Thema Serendipity,” in *Archithese*, 6.2010.
- Charles W. Sutton (ed.), *Transactions of the Lancashire and Cheshire Antiquarian Society*, vol. IV, 1886, p. 289.
- “Wolfsziegel,” https://de.wikipedia.org/wiki/Wolfsziegel.

Astrid Staufer, The Klanghaus as an “Experiment”
- Hermann Czech, *Ungefähre Hauptrichtung. Schriften und Gespräche zur Architektur*, Vienna, 2021.
- Hermann Czech, *Zur Abwechslung: Ausgewählte Schriften zur Architektur in Wien*, Vienna, 1996.
- Andreas Nierhaus and Peter Husty (eds.), *Johann Bernhard Fischer von Erlach*, Vienna, 2023.
- Juhani Pallasmaa, *The Eyes of the Skin*, Los Angeles, 1996.
- Christian Zehnder, *Triohotala*, https://www.new-space-mountain.ch/10332617/music.

Image credits

Front endpaper
- © Peter Roth, *Psalm 121*, *Psalm 148*.

Photographs
- PP. 1, 3, 5–8
  © Ladina Bischof.
- PP. 2, 4,
  © Ueli Steingruber.

Thesis Competition
- P. 17, fig. 1
  © Roland Bernath.
- PP. 18–27
  Marcel Meili, *Thesis Competition*, 2010.

Sabine von Fischer. Annäherungen an den Klang
- P. 29, fig. 1
  © Staufer & Hasler Architekten.
- P. 33, fig. 2
  © Staufer & Hasler Architekten.

Axel Langer. Holes in the Wall
- P. 37, fig. 1
  © Marcel Meili, photo of model from thesis competition, 2010.
- P. 37, fig. 2
  © Peter Röllin.
- P. 38, fig. 3
  Germanisches Nationalmuseum, Nuremberg, MI574.
- P. 38, fig. 4
  Germanisches Nationalmuseum, Nuremberg, Drawing of MI574.
- P. 38, figs. 5–6
  Austrian National Library, Cod. Mixt. 1594.
- P. 41, fig. 7
  © MehmetO / Alamy Stock Photo.
- P. 41, fig. 8
  Jointly owned by The Metropolitan Museum of Art and The Arthur M. Sackler Museum, Harvard University; Gift from Mr. and Mrs. Stuart Cary Welch Jr., 1988 © bpk / The Metropolitan Museum of Art.
- P. 41, fig. 9
  © Matyas Rehak / Alamy Stock Photo.
- P. 41, fig. 10
  © Staufer & Hasler Architekten with Applied Acoustics.
- P. 42, fig. 11
  Germanisches Nationalmuseum, Nuremberg, MIR718.
- P. 42, fig. 12
  Kelsey Museum of Archaeology, 1971.1.22.
- P. 42, fig. 13
  © Dreamstime.
- P. 42, fig. 14
  Germanisches Nationalmuseum, Nuremberg, MIR731.
- P. 42, fig. 15
  The Bodleian Libraries, University of Oxford, MP. Elliot 251.

Eva Kuss. A Built Resonator
- P. 45, fig. 1
  © Staufer & Hasler Architekten.
- P. 45, fig. 2
  © Ralph Brühwiler.
- P. 46, figs. 3–4
  © Staufer & Hasler Architekten, Robin Möhl.
- P. 46, figs. 5–8
  © Roland Bernath.
- P. 49, fig. 9
  © Roland Bernath.
- P. 49, fig. 10
  © Ralph Brühwiler.
- P. 49, fig. 11
  © Staufer & Hasler Architekten.
- P. 49, fig. 12
  © Roland Bernath.
- P. 49, figs. 13–14
  © Ralph Brühwiler.
- P. 50, figs. 15–20
  © Roland Bernath.

Matthias Ruf. An Accessible Instrument
- P. 55, figs. 1–2
  © Staufer & Hasler Architekten, 2024.
- P. 55, fig. 3
  J.-M. Fontaine, *Étude des vases acoustiques disposés dans les églises du XI–XVIII siècles.* Dissertation at CNAM, Paris, 1979.
- P. 55, fig. 4
  Athanasius Kircher, *Neue Hall- und Thon-Kunst. Oder Mechanische Gehaim-Verbindung der Kunst und Natur*, 1684, pp. 22 & 67.
- P. 55, fig. 5
  © Staufer & Hasler Architekten, 2024.
- P. 56, fig. 6
  Aline Kottmann, *St. Walburga in Meschede. Der karolingische Bau und das Schalltopfensemble*, Büchenbach, 2015.
- P. 56, fig. 7
  Regine Abegg and Christine Barraud Wiener, *Kunstdenkmäler des Kantons Zürich*, new edition, vol. II, Bern, 2002.
- P. 56, figs. 8–9
  Charles W. Sutton (ed.), *Transactions of the Lancashire and Cheshire Antiquarian Society*, vol. IV, 1886, Manchester, p. 289.
- P. 56, figs. 10a–10b
  Source: https://de.wikipedia.org/wiki/Wolfsziegel, http://www.windmusik.com/html/wolftile.htm (accessed on March 24, 2024).
- P. 58, fig. 11
  © Metal workshop, David Fuchs, Deggenhausen, 2013.
- P. 58, fig. 12
  © Metal workshop, David Fuchs, Deggenhausen, 1981.
- P. 58, figs. 13–16
  © Andres Bosshard, 1987.
- P. 61, figs. 17–18
  © Metal workshop, David Fuchs, Deggenhausen, 2023.
- P. 61, fig. 19
  © Metal workshop, David Fuchs, Deggenhausen, 2013.
- P. 61, figs. 20–21
  © Metal workshop, David Fuchs, Deggenhausen, 2023.
- P 61, fig. 22
  © Metal workshop, David Fuchs, Deggenhausen, 2024.
- PP. 62–69
  Sectional perspectives based on 3D construction drawings by timber builders and joiners, Andrea Dell'Ambrogio, Laura Martinel with Matthias Ruf.

Andrea Wiegelmann. An Essentially Social Project
- P. 71, fig. 1
  © Ralph Brühwiler.
- P. 74, fig. 2
  © Staufer & Hasler Architekten.
- P. 77, fig. 3
  © IG Klanghaus Toggenburg, Screenshot Facebook
- P. 78, figs. 4–6
  © Roland Bernath.

Christian Gressbach. In Search of Resonance
- P. 84, fig. 1
  © Herzog & de Meuron and Studio Noun.
- P. 84, fig. 2
  © Peter Roth.
- P. 84, fig. 3
  © Herzog & de Meuron and Studio Noun.

Sound Maps
- PP. 86–87
  © Staufer & Hasler Architekten mit Andres Bosshard, 2024.

Alfred Messerli. Songs from the Heart
- P. 89, fig. 1
  Vermischte lieder vor den land-mann, first page, 1779.
- P. 91, fig. 2
  Franz Niklaus, Josef Reinhard, *Ulrich und Salome Bräker*, Vernis mou, um 1801.

Klangweg
- P. 93, figs. 3–8
  © Beat Belser.

Lea Hagmann. In Harmony with Nature
- P. 95, fig. 1
  © Staufer & Hasler Architekten, Robin Möhl.
- P. 96, fig. 2
  © Ralph Brühwiler.
- P. 99, fig. 3
  © Ralph Brühwiler.
- P. 100, fig. 4
  © Ralph Brühwiler.

Susanna Koeberle. The Material Vitality of Shingles
- P. 103, figs. 1–2
  © Staufer & Hasler Architekten, Robin Möhl.
- P. 104, figs. 3–4
  © Ralph Brühwiler.
- P. 105, figs. 5–6
  © Ralph Brühwiler.
- P. 106, fig. 7
  © Staufer & Hasler Architekten, Robin Möhl.
- P. 106, fig. 8
  © Staufer & Hasler Architekten.

Photographs
- PP. 108–117
  © Ladina Bischof.

Astrid Staufer, The Klanghaus as an "Experiment"
- P. 123, fig. 1
  © Staufer & Hasler Architekten.
- P. 123, fig. 2
  © Martin Feiersinger, "Pavillons—Casinos—Follies. Eine zeichnerische Annäherung", in Andreas Nierhaus and Peter Husty (eds.), *Johann Bernhard Fischer von Erlach*, Vienna, 2023, pp. 65–73.
- P. 124, fig. 3
  © Visualization Nightnurse Images 2013.
- P. 125, figs. 4–5
  © Staufer & Hasler Architekten.
- P. 126, fig. 6
  © Christian Zehnder, *Triohotala*, filmstill, https://www.new-space-mountain.ch/10332617/music.
- P. 126, fig. 7
  © Roland Bernath.
- P. 127, figs. 8–9
  © Roland Bernath.

Responsible Project Participants
- P. 130, fig. 1
  © Ralph Brühwiler.

Photographs
- PP. 137–144
  © Ueli Steingruber.

Back endpaper
- © Christian Zehnder *Soundline 1*, *Soundline 2*.

Resonances: Klanghaus Toggenburg

Editors	Erol Doguoglu, Mirjam Fischer, and Astrid Staufer
Concept	Mirjam Fischer, Astrid Staufer
Managing editor	Mirjam Fischer
Translations	Rupert Hebblethwaite
Copyediting	Sören Davy, Melissa Larner
Proofreading	Michaela Alex-Eibensteiner
Project coordination	Mirjam Fischer, mille pages
Photography	Roland Bernath, Ladina Bischof, Ralph Brühwiler, Ueli Steingruber
Design	Norm, Zurich
Printing	merkur medien, Langenthal
Binding	Buchbinderei Grollimund AG, Reinach
Paper	Werkdruck 1.5 Weiss, 150g/m²
Font	atak, semibold, outofthedark.swiss

Lars Müller Publishers is supported by the Swiss Federal Office of Culture with a structural contribution for the years 2021–25.

Lars Müller Publishers
Zurich, Switzerland
info@lars-muller.ch
www.lars-mueller-publishers.com
+41 44 274 37 40

Product safety
Producer: Lars Müller Publishers GmbH
Pfingstweidstrasse 6, 8005 Zurich, Switzerland
Responsible person in accordance with EU Regulation 2023/988 (GPSR): Michael Klein, sales representative, Hub 1, DE-84149 Velden
+49 8742 964 552 2, gpsr@lars-muller.ch

English edition ISBN 978-3-03778-786-1
German edition ISBN 978-3-03778-787-8

Distributed in North America, Latin America, and the Caribbean by ARTBOOK | D.A.P.
www.artbook.com

First edition
Printed in Switzerland

Kanton St.Gallen
Hochbauamt

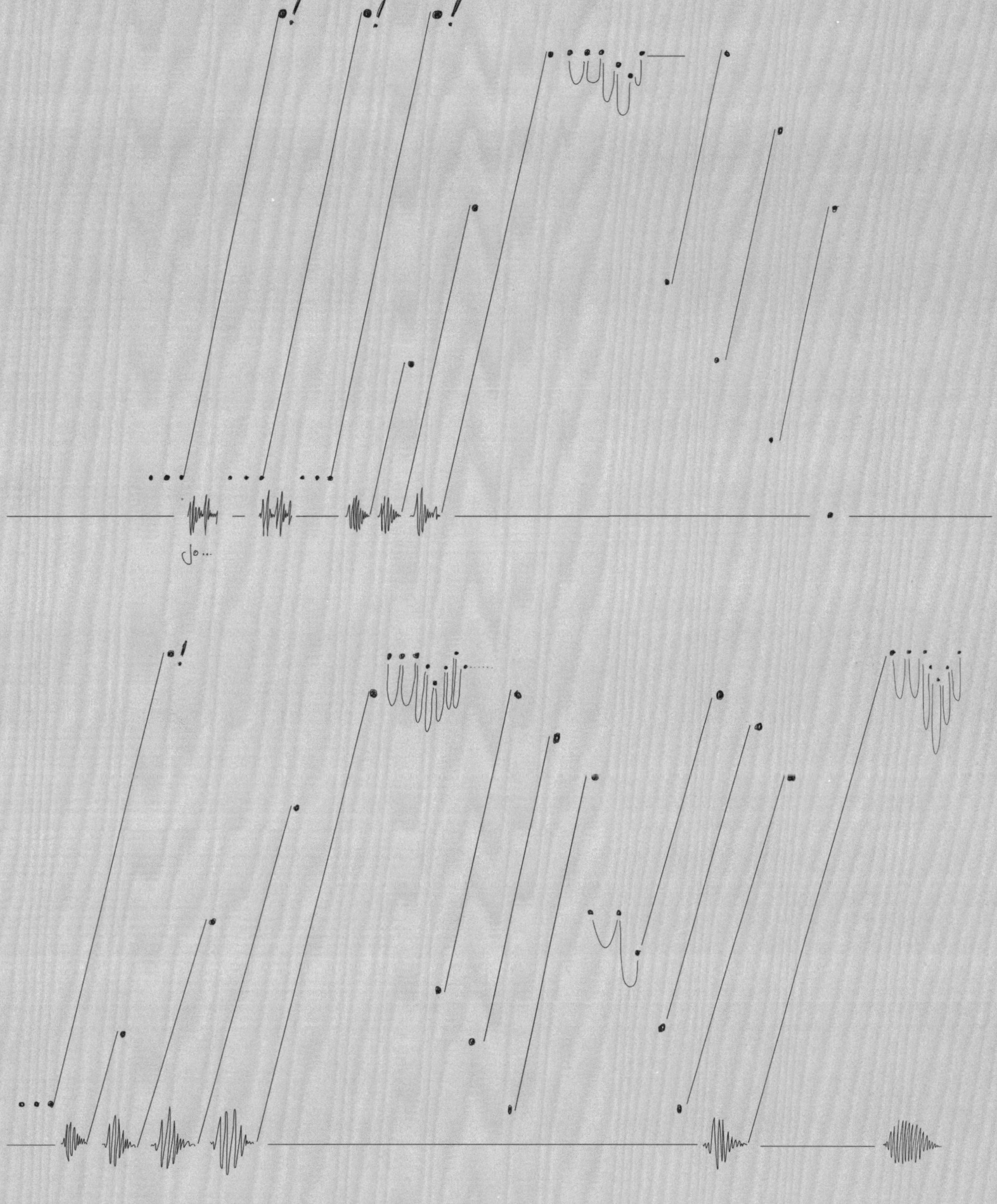

Christian Zehnder, *Soundline 1—Evening Call*
Recorded in the central space of the Klanghaus with two echo cushions.

Christian Zehnder, *Soundline 2—Morning Call (Dedicated to Schwendisee)*
Recorded in the central space of the Klanghaus, in front of an acoustic mirror.